AN INDUSTRY WORTH FIGHTING FOR

By Derrick Josi

With Steve Olivas

Edited by Allyson Brooks

Print ISBN: 9-781-956-577-006
Ebook ISBN: 9-781-956-577-013

There is a cult of ignorance in the United States, and there has always been. The strain of anti-intellectualism has been a constant thread winding its way through our political and cultural life, nurtured by the false notion that democracy means that "my ignorance is just as good as your knowledge."
~ Isaac Asimov

An industry that feeds you is an industry worth fighting for.
~ Tierra Kessler

Table of Contents

Prologue

It took me awhile to figure out how I was going to start this book. I wasn't sure of how to introduce all the concerns and ideas that raced through my mind. Where do I start? What exactly do I want to say? How do I say it?

As I sorted my feelings and my knowledge, I did what we all tend to do. I absently picked up my phone and opened it.

I had received a couple of disturbing screenshots from a farmer friend of mine. The content was a private Instagram message they received from a dubious account. The purpose of the account was to publicly shame dairy farmers. The account was called "Commit Suicide Losers." It also carried the username (or "@") "kill.yourself.you.are.pathetic."

The actual verbiage of the message was blunt and to the point:

Kill yourself. You're disgusting.
You can't even say anything.
Scared Weakling. You're pathetic.
Commit suicide.
Loser.
You are a terrible Liar.
Kill yourself.

I wasn't too surprised by the abusive attitude in the messages. I deal with this kind of angry belittlement nearly every day. It isn't always this horrific, but it's pretty common to find online flames, insults, and slurs aimed at dairy farmers. We encounter a constant barrage of condemnation from those who feel the undying need to explain just how awful they think the industry is. They drill home their righteous indignation, declaring that dairy farming irreparably damages both cows and humans. The tone ranges from broad generalizations to unnervingly personal accusations.

Honestly, I don't know where these people find the time. It is hard to imagine they could be gainfully employed, raise a family, run a household, and have any semblance of a social life, and still find the free time to devote to such an invasive hobby. It seems these self-authorized folks endlessly scroll Facebook, TikTok, Twitter, and any other social media sites, pick out every post they disagree with, and then respond with an ill-informed diatribe.

One thing is quite clear: they certainly don't feel the need to waste time by doing any viable research, nor do they bother with vetting their facts. All they need is a phone, an agenda, and all the time in the world.

I read those screenshots sent by my farmer friend. I reflected on how these messages made me shrug my shoulders, grunt in frustration, and shake my head, all at the same time. Here it was, in the reflexive action of just looking at my phone and feeling an instinctual frustration that I found my starting point.

I will share these social media encounters to show what drives me to be a champion for the everyday, independent dairy farmer. It is what I'm passionate about.

However, I will spare the reader the worst of the worst, the messages dripping with blood and savagery aimed at my wife or my three-year-old daughter. Entertaining such cruelty is a slippery slope, and I will not stoop to that level. Instead, I report those posts to the social media overlords, and they do their duty to pursue the worst offenders.

So far, there has been only one instance where the local police needed to be notified. That message was particularly specific, and the situation would have ended badly for the offender had they shown up on my property.

Another reason I will not share those posts is because, honestly, I don't save them. I have no reason to revisit such disturbing content. No one needs that extreme level of negativity in life.

I allow the less-threatening folks to hang around my social media pages for as long as they want or until they pass a certain threshold of annoying, disturbing, or disgusting. At that point, I quietly block them and move on with my life. I genuinely don't need to block many people. I think the world should see them for who they are. More importantly, I want everyone else to see my replies. Some days I have more time and energy than others. After all, I am gainfully employed, and I am co-raising a family, co-running a household, and trying to maintain a little bit of a social life. But I take whatever time is necessary to reply to each message as they come in. It's the least I can do to stand up for my industry.

Social media can be a powerful force of good in life, but it can also give a bullhorn to the worst of human impulses. Most of the messages I receive are written by "activists" who use emotion and manipulation in the hope of getting under my skin. They fail; I respond with common sense and straightforward knowledge. Also, I can dispel a lot of misinformation by communicating back and forth in public messaging.

I'm hoping you've noticed the quotation marks I put around the word "activist," too. When I think of a true activist, I think of people who advocate for beneficial change, who have a clear understanding of the problem and the solution, and who work to make allies instead of enemies. I think of people like Jimmy Carter, Johnny "Appleseed" Chapman, John Mellencamp, and George Washington Carver. People who worked hard, met others face-to-face, spoke to the public respectfully, and were never afraid to get their hands dirty. These are true activists. And I'm proud to say that the dairy industry has numerous activists and activist organizations that not only support us farmers, but keep us honest, too.

My intention is to bring you the truth; the truth about dairy farming. This is my truth, straight from my experience, my upbringing, and my knowledge. I'm not perfect, and I'd never claim to be. I'm pretty sure there are other dairy farmers out there who know a heck of a lot more than I do (and I'd love to talk to them!). A lot of folks out there who are not dairy farmers have a lot to say about dairy farming. That's fine. All I ask is that you approach my truth with an open mind, and remember the words of Andy Rooney: "People will generally accept facts as truth only if the facts agree with what they already believe."

Here is a smattering of examples I've encountered online. I show them here verbatim; nothing has been altered. These are in no particular order of time, intensity, or topic.

***

> *I don't mind you moving cows around, But sending cows to slaughter at the end of there life is disgusting and in Christian. Slaughtering is very painful for cows and other animals. I want every slaughterhouse put out of Business.*

Using a religious angle is a common ploy used by activists. They suppress and exclude information, or cherry-pick small bits and pieces of their faith to fit a narrow point of view. They don't remember that slaughtering or sacrificing livestock was mentioned repeatedly in the Bible. These were customary practices back then, and are made far more humane and painless today. Slaughter and euthanasia will be addressed in Chapter Six.

Because there's nothing honest about them! Like all farming organisations, they keep their cruel methods hidden and away from public eyes.

This one raised my left eyebrow.

Another gimmick is to be vague and mysterious. The storyteller warns of something ominous and unseen behind a door and in the shadows. They won't say what is exactly back there, but they want you to feel the hair on the back of your neck stand up. It's no ordinary conspiracy theory; it is pure, insistent paranoia.

3

My farm holds numerous tours and inspections for visitors, school groups, dairy professionals, government and organizational inspectors, auditors, and agents every year. I guess some people think I have two sets of barns on my property: one set I allow the public to view, and another set where I do the actual dirty work. They perceive it as a secret lair where I commit atrocities against bovinity and humanity alike.

People who have no ability to critically think through the information we give are the ones who imagine these clandestine dairy practices. The reality is that there is no practical way I could keep anything hidden from public eyes. Those eyes are everywhere!

How mean clamping there ears the just babies shame on you…

Other people will pick out one aspect of dairy farming and hone in on that. The person will try to manipulate the reader's emotions instead of using any valid reasoning.

I've got to admit, this one took me a moment or so to decipher. The writer is referring to ear tags. We hang a tag which looks like a plastic earring on each calf to help identify them. The tags are numbered, which helps ensure that every cow has all of their needs met. We have a database that tracks milking, breeding, illness, and anything else we need to know about the calf. With hundreds of cows running around, we need a reliable method to keep up with each individual.

Just to be clear: Yes, there is a moment of pain when we first insert the tag. It's exactly like when a human gets their ears pierced, which, by the way, is an extremely common practice. We go through cartilage, which is much less painful than if we went through muscle and flesh.

Why don't you hook all that shit up to your own tits! See how that feels!

I actually chuckled a little at this. The writer is referring to the milking machine. I describe the process in detail later in this book. The quick version: suction tubes are placed over the cow's teats (like the nipples on human beings) and their udder is pumped for milk.

Sound familiar?

Any woman who has breastfed a newborn has most likely pumped her breasts between feedings. That relieves pressure in the mother's breasts, and it also creates a supply of mother's milk that is now available when Dad gets up at two a.m. to feed the little one.

In any case, my reply to the writer was that I have personally never hooked that "shit" up to my own "tits," but my wife has done it many times.

4

Disgusting people you hopefully you'll be shut down.

Some messages are just random, unprovoked attacks. Someone will just attack me instead of addressing the problem itself. The syntax on this one was curious to me. It was as if the writer had several competing thoughts in their head and mashed two of them together as they came out.

There are most definitely coordinated attacks on animal farm pages, because there needs to be. To expose dairy for what it is: cruel and unnecessary. We want you to feel the pressure of what you are doing is wrong and unethical. We are a voice for the animals. It's simple. NO reason to get all bent outta shape about it and start making fake
comments. Start farming plants instead and you won't have any problems.

As you can see, this one of the more ominous messages; ones that act as thinly veiled threats. They sound like a mob boss talking to a small business owner, implying that bad things could happen if you don't pay protection money to my guy on the first of every month. In other words, do what we want, and nothing bad might accidentally happened to you.

I've been blocked despite only engaging in educated challenging no offensive behavior. Feel free to light them up.

To my eye, this also seems like a call to action. It enables others to engage in aggressive behavior. I'm not sure how else you could read that.

I have a question for you Mr farmer. Do you see humans as inherently superior to non-human animals, and hence deserving of certain objectification and treatment?
I ask as a rational argument can be drawn out that would describe that as the arbitrary discrimination known as speciesism. That concept relies on acknowledging differential treatment based on non-relevant characteristics lacks moral justification. The same logic that applies that other forms of arbitrary discrimination such as racism, sexism, ableism, etc, that we know lacks justification.
Sure we can talk about the nitty gritty of the treatment and the supposed humaneness of it all, but I am asking you about first principles, the initial justification.

Goodness! Sounds like someone got a shiny, new thesaurus for their birthday!

5

I occasionally find a replier who attempts to sound smart using a lot of "fifty-cent words." What the replier didn't know is that the more complex the writing, the more incompetent the writer comes across. A professor at Princeton University ran some experiments that involved participants reading a paragraph of needlessly complicated text; afterward, the people judged the writer to lack intelligence (Oppenheimer, 2005). So, it's not just me saying this—it's science.

But, all snark aside: this replier has no intention of having an adult discussion with me. The replier is hoping to intimidate me with defeasible reasoning and obfuscated vernacular (see? I can do it, too!). Obviously, it didn't work.

Just because I'm a dairy farmer doesn't mean I'm stupid.

You're a dairey farmer. So you take the babys off the mothers, so you can sell the milk,This is true.The mother cows mourns there stolen babys. The stolen babys cry endlessly for there mothers. Females go in to the dairy industry to suffer the same fait,. The males go for veal or are killed .All dairey cows are sent to slaughter when there bodyscarnt take any more,a round 5 or 6 years old . This is all true FACT. Are you going to block me now? Because wot I'm say is true and your only protecting you bank account. No one sends a loved animal to a slaughter house.

This post brings up a common and emotionally-charged theme: the welfare of cows and calves.

Some people have a problem with slaughter houses. I can get on board with the moral arguments surrounding them. Any aspect of death, especially the death of an animal, is frightening to think of. The blood and gore associated with an animal's demise in a slaughterhouse is even more terrifying to think about.

Others have a problem with separating calves from their mothers. I understand that, too. We set a high store on the bond between mother and child. This particular issue I will address later in Chapter Two.

The writers of those comments do have an anchor for their position. It comes from their heart and sense of compassion. The problem is, these people cannot step away from their emotions long enough to do just a smidge of common-sense research about it.

Let's talk about horse breeding. The big horse farms breed their horses every 9 months in hopes of getting a winning horse. It done same as cows. That to me is sad some rejects are sold others sent to killed for meat. Cows are meant to give milk and eat.

Ignoring the obvious inconsistency of simultaneously being offended that cows are sent to be killed for meat, and that cows are meant to give milk and eat (maybe they meant cows should just eat and provide milk), I replied with a simple fact:

Horses carry a foal for 11 months so they can't be bred every nine months (Espy, 2016).

How hard would that have been to look that up? It wasn't for me. And why do I have to do all the work for these morons, anyway? It would help their cause to at least get their facts straight before they come at me.

Everyone is an expert, I suppose. Why let the facts get in the way of your argument?

Why did she have a pacifier in her mouth at her age she seems to love to talk can't do it with that

I will also get the occasional parenting expert. This one came to me after posting a video of my 18-month old daughter toddling around with a pacifier in her mouth. My first reaction was to write, "Yeah, but at your age, you should be able to write a sentence properly."

But I didn't. I took the high road. I said what I always say—which is some version of "Leave the parenting of my children to me."We live in a world where people feel compelled to correct everyone around them. Consider the miserable life they must lead, always focused on everyone else's faults.

"How can you, as a mother, allow these atrocities to happen?"
"You have no empathy. You are one cold bitch."
"You must be broken as a woman."
"You are a terrible mother and a horrible example to your poor children."
"What if these were your children?"
"Would you slaughter your babies?"

This is a list that can go on forever. From what I have learned from talking with farmers all over the country is that female farmers get attacked more viciously than male farmers. Male dairy farmers are simply labeled as monsters. Female dairy farmers, however, are vilified as turning their backson motherhood and femininity. They are an insult to any woman's instinctual maternal nature. They are worse than monsters.

***

I'm sure I sound bitter, but I really don't mean to.

It's easy to get swept up in the irritation of thinking idiots make up a large number of the people on the internet. Thirty years ago, if 100 outraged irrational zealots around the world made themselves known, they would be completely isolated and dismissed by normal people that had a firm grasp on reality. Now, those 100 people find each other online, band together, and form a coordinated swarm to attack, making it seem as if they numbered in the millions.

Unfortunately, these online attackers never realize that the way they present themselves immediately discredits them. I've seen evidence of this, especially when they make really obvious mistakes. Once in awhile, one of them will share my content to one of their groups on Facebook. However, they don't have the group profile set to "private mode." So I get a front row seat to read everything that gets said. And, it's evident that their content was not meant to be seen by me.

It's both sad and hilarious to read their posts.They create convoluted schemes to spread misinformation.They discuss how to crop pictures or videos to bend my own words around their narrative. It's like a comedy of errors, starring Dr. Evil as he tries to weaponize a bunch of Scooby Doo villains.

And they would've gotten away with it, too, if it wasn't for those meddling farmers!

The most illuminating part is when one of them proclaims, "Yeah! I replied to him from all six of my accounts!" Creating multiple fake accounts is a big problem on Facebook. This is how these groups take their small number of members and inflate it by having each member create multiple accounts. The VP of Facebook, Guy Rosen, released a report saying they disabled more than 1.3 billion fake accounts between October and December of 2020 (Rosen, 2021). But, they still have a long way to go.

Another way they discredit themselves is sloppy, lazy posting. I will receive the same message, with the same typos, bad grammar, and delusional misrepresentationfrom multiple accounts. Apparently, they don't have time to come up with several versions of the same tired insults, so they just cut and paste from one fake account to the next.

They may assume I don't read all the comments, so they figure they can get away with it. Their motive is not about education, reality, or truth—it's about forming an attack swarm. The swarm technique would be brilliant if the swarmers weren't so sloppy.

8

Online activists fight awfully hard to convince you that what you see with your own eyes and ears is false. As for me, my videos are simple and to the point. Truth stands on its own merit.

***

It ain't easy, folks. I have a thick skin. These negative messages represent only two or three percent of all the words that pour into my inbox and onto my social media feeds. There are a ton of wonderful and positive messages I receive from fans and from everyday folks who learn from my posts and videos. They give me kindness and support, and they appreciate the peek inside the world of dairy.

Tell you what. Let me start from the start. Go ahead; throw a couple more logs onto the fire, grab some hot cocoa, and kick back with the kids. Of course, I'll tell you all I know about the dairy industry. But first, I'll give you the story of how it all began for me, Derrick Josi, on Facebook.

Chapter 1
Taking the Plunge

These days, I think it would be safe to say that I am a notable social influencer when it comes to dairy farming. There are some enormous accounts that talk about farming in general, but I'm probably in the top ten of dairy farming. I'm happy to bear that burden—and make no mistake, it is quite a burden at times. Throughout I'll show the challenges I face from an online perspective. Fortunately, the critics really do represent a tiny fraction of the amazing interactions I have online every day. Almost all of these interactions are with perfect strangers who are curious, fascinated, and kind.

But the real story here is the day-to-day operational issues facing dairy farmers as they conduct everyday business. The care and handling of over 500 living animals (and it may grow to 1,000 by the time this book is published) makes each day a symphony of organized chaos.

Many of my vlogs (short for video log, a kind of online visual diary) on Facebook and Instagram are made to pull back the curtain and shine a light on exactly what it's like to bring you the best dairy products on the planet. I think it would help to give some insight as to why I chose to dabble on social media in the first place. I'm still amazed as to how I grew to be a big farm account on Facebook.

It probably has to do with how amazingly good-looking I am.

At least, that's the story I tell myself.

***

It began on a rainy Sunday in November of 2016. I walked through the Portland airport, weary from a long and irritating flight—but my mind was buzzing with ideas after the National Milk conference. More formally, it's called The Annual Meeting of the National Milk Producers Federation.   A quick tutorial: the NMPF is an organization founded to lobby Washington DC lawmakers on behalf of American dairy farmers. Their mission, as listed on their webpage (www.nmpf.org) is, "...to foster an economic and political climate in which dairy producers and the cooperatives they own can thrive and prosper." They speak on our collective behalf and create a political voice for many independent farms and farmers.

In other words, these guys are the true activists for us.

I try to attend every year. I am a small business owner and have a vested interest in how the blustery winds of politics are going to affect my farm. The year 2016 was no exception. During that year's conference, I sat through a rather interesting seminar.

The program I watched was put on by a man named Don Schindler, a digital strategist who was contracted by the NMPF to help thrust farmers into the age of digital media.

You might ask yourself why a dairy farmer would care one way or the other about platforms like Twitter or Tik Tok, and the answer might surprise you. Don's explanation was simple: farmers need to create a business webpage and a social media presence.

Why?

1. To more fluidly network with other farmers. Ideas, problems, and solutions can be shared on the public forum of social media in such a way that helping one farmer will help many. We become a nationwide co-op where we can gather and talk shop.

2. The NMPF was eager for farmers to tell their stories online. They wanted to educate consumers and bring the industry to life by using a medium that would reach the most people. For me, that means younger people. Farmers are an aging bunch. It is getting to be nearly impossible to attract younger people to farming as a career.

3. To help people gain an appreciation for what we do. Heck, it's important to have people understand where their food comes from. As shocking as it sounds, a gallon of milk doesn't just magically appear at your local grocery store. There is a lot of farm work involved from a typical a farmer like me. And I am only the tip of the spear.

4. Finally, and more nefariously, Don spoke of needing to get ahead of potential under-handed online activities conducted by so-called "activist" groups intent on hurting the industry. In his example, if a news event casts a farm or farmer in a bad light (say, abuse allegations or an accident that resulted in an injury or death), one of the delusionist groups could then open a website or social media account posing as the farmer (or a farm spokesperson). They could then blast out incorrect information aimed at further disparaging the individual farm/farmer—or more likely, the industry as a whole.

This point resonated with me. I had been online with my personal social media accounts for quite awhile by 2016. As you can imagine, I had absolutely noticed a trend of online trolls spreading false rumors—and outright lies—about the industry. Sometimes, they would blatantly post erroneous information. The more determined ones would selectively crop a photo or video clip, and then add a voiceover or caption that would mislead by inference.

Those kinds of people drive me nuts. I don't understand the urge to win people over by using sensationalism and dishonesty. In my world, you give somebody the information and let them make a decision based upon the evidence shown and their point of view. Grandpa Ernie taught me that.

My guess is that people who lie (especially to lure more followers or supporters) know very clearly that nobody would take their side if all the correct information were available. In other words, because their side doesn't make sense, they have to distort the truth and show it in small, short bursts. That way, people who don't want to put the legwork into researching the real answers will be duped. They'll get sucked in like they're caught in a tractor beam.

Don't get me started.

Hold on…that's exactly what got me started.

Don Schindler didn't pick me specifically. As I mentioned, he charged the entire industry to get on board with the 21st century. I had a couple advantages over some of my aging counterparts when it came to developing a real online presence. First, I was younger. I understood the basic tenants of social media and was already fluent in how Facebook worked. I didn't have much knowledge on algorithms or UXD, but I could navigate a site with little difficulty.

Secondly, I wasn't afraid to get up and speak in front of people. That means speaking at live events (like the seminar Don put on), but also speaking out online. I wouldn't say I'm fearless with regard to the things I address and take on as a vlogger, but I do not hesitate when it comes to telling the truth. You want someone who will stand up against the onslaught of detrimental misinformation? I'm your guy!

I drove home from the airport in silence. My wife, Kaycee, had been with me on the trip. She was tired and didn't say much in the car. That was okay—I liked the quiet. I didn't even want the radio to interfere with the ideas jumping around my head like popcorn.

When we got home, I parked the car in the driveway and went into the house. Just like I do every time I come home, I walked through the front door and began to unlace my boots.

Kaycee went directly to the bedroom to shower off the travel residue that seems to cling to you in every airport and every airplane. On her way to shower, she asked what I wanted to do for dinner. I think I said something about ordering in. I had other things on my mind.

I wanted to get to work.

***

I didn't know a heck of a lot about growing as a social media influencer. Honestly, I had no intention of growing into a big account. I just wanted to continue doing what I could to get the word out. I wanted to combat the erroneous notions that were being spread by organizations and people that had an agenda to destroy the industry I loved.

Every farmer online has had numerous experiences arguing with imbeciles online. I was no exception. Random false information, and the zealots who buy into the rhetoric, pop up from time to time. I had already woven a little back-and-forth into my personal page. I was on fire to begin integrating Don Schindler's message into my personal social media. But my focus was eclipsed by the daily chores and workload of running the farm.

However, a single event catapulted me into action. In November of 2016, someone I knew in Tillamook shared an anti-dairy shock video on their social media pageand declared they were "...DONE with dairy."

My heart dropped into my stomach. This was someone I knew. That person lived smack-dab in the middle of an area that was built by dairy farming. Tillamook is obviously the dairy capital of the world (don't argue with me about this). The climate and the soil make farming easier here than many other parts of the country. As a result, farms (and dairy farms) exist everywhere around here.

How could someone who knows first-hand exactly how much hard work and sacrifice goes into farming be swayed by this propaganda? How could someone who grew up around farming fall prey to this? They should know reality versus fiction. They've lived it.

As I type this, I still can't wrap my head around it.

But there it was on screen.

The video is well-known in the dairy farming community. It's called Dairy is Scary, and has been in existence since 2015. The narrator's channel has received millions of views as she capitalizes on sensationalizing her version of dairy farming. The creator's goal was to take a lot of common practices on dairy farms and portray them in the worst possible light, all in an effort to paint dairy farmers as cold, sadistic brutes.

Seeing that video for the first time along with my friend's comment was a watershed moment for me. I was shocked that a fellow dairy farmer who lived near me, in the middle of a dairy community, would be willing to watch that video and believe it! I was further stunned when they declared that they were now an enemy of dairy farmers, and called for the farms to be shut down.

This was wrong. Something had to change.Somebody needed to actually put themselves out there.

I don't want to sound like I was the first person to ever think of this. It was late 2016 and social media platforms had been around for quite awhile. A number of people had already created content to advocate for the dairy farming industry. Their mission was to speak the truth and educate consumers about the industry.

I wanted to take a different approach from what I had seen online. I wanted to be more direct with my delivery. My personality isn't wired to deliver a soft tap on the shoulder to consumers. My voice is much stronger, and much more in your face. It was time to stop pulling punches.

You want sunshine and rainbows? Keep moving. You want the reality as it is lived every day, by every dairy farmer doing their job, seven days per week? Then I'm your guy.

I set out to expand my page. I wanted to broaden the "informational" side of my online presence. I initially thought an anonymous account might be the best way to accomplish that. Everyone else does it. Surely I would be able to anonymously post online. Right?

Nah.

The "anonymous" side of the account lasted all of two days. Tillamook is a small community. Whenever I would "anonymously" post a photo of the landscape or of the farm, most of my community knew it was me. After you've been around this area for awhile, you know exactly what everything looks like and who everybody is. Not to mention, if I posted photos of my cows, other farmers could tell it was me by their ear tags.

So much for that idea. But I was not to be dissuaded.The decision to proceed as Derrick Josi was a pretty easy one. I switched my tactic and began to post as myself.

I started out as a blogger. I did some research on how other influential farmers delivered their message, and writing a regular online diary blog seemed to be the most common medium. I tried that route, posting a picture with each entry.Yet, as for anyone who has seen my two- or three-minute video vlogs, you can guess how I felt about sitting down and writing a column a couple times per week.

I hated it.

"Hate" is probably too strong of a word, but writing a standard blog didn't suit me. I don't have a lot of time to devote to things outside of farm and family, so I found the process to be tedious and too time consuming.

Not to mention, the modern consumer rarely takes the time to read a full blog entry. We have become a country of watchers and listeners rather than readers. It's not really a bad thing; we're all busy and have to make decisions with regard to how we allocate our time. Thus, I had to look at new technology for new opportunities.

The next step in my online evolution was to create a strategy of hybrid written and visual content. I started to take pictures, adding a caption explaining what the viewer was seeing, and posting those online.

Not long after that, the light bulb went off in my head. I figured out that it's way easier to talk about things than it is to write about them. I began to shoot short videos and post those. In less than one year, I had evolved from columnist/blogger, to video content creator.

By the autumn of 2017, I had found my modus operandi.

My methods, by the way, are constantly evolving. I pay close attention to what works best for me on each social media platform (Facebook, especially). In order to gain the maximum distribution of a video, it helps to be somewhat in tune with the algorithm Facebook uses.

I know you hear the word "algorithm" all the time. It sounds like a scary math term that your 12th grade calculus teacher used to freak everyone out before a big exam. It's an intimidating term. To put it very simply, the Facebook algorithm is just an extensive set of mathematical calculations (Custard, 2021).

This is how the Facebook algorithm works, according to Facebook:

1. The algorithm will take all the posts in a user's network of friends and followers and score them according to certain factors like the type of post, its recency, and so on.

2. It will get rid of posts that the user is unlikely to pay attention to, based on their past activity. It also downgrades clickbait, misinformation, and anything the user specifically says they don't want to see.

3. It then runs a "more powerful neural network" through what's left. It will score those posts in a more personalized way and rank them in order of their value. For instance, if Frieda is more likely to "like" a funny cow meme, she'll see more cow content. If she's less likely to comment on her aunt's latest interpretive dance video, she'll see less dance content.

4. Finally, it puts together a nice mélange of media and source material for the user to scroll through. (Custard, 2021; Lada, Wang, and Yan, 2021)

In a nutshell, the Facebook algorithm customizes each user's feed individually. What shows up in the feed is dependent on what the user engages with. So I try to tailor my videos to best suit my followers' viewing habits.

Another thing I have to be aware of was the content itself. And managing that content can be a real big burr under my saddle. Both of Facebook's Terms of Service and Community Standards are written in plain, non-legal-sounding language, and they tell you what you can and cannot post. They also go over what will happen if you violate those terms.

This particular rule for Facebook posting is the one that affects me the most:

For the following content, we include a warning screen so that people are aware the content may be disturbing. We also limit the ability to view the content to adults, ages 18 and older:

Imagery of Animals

As we know, farm life isn't always the prettiest thing to see. It comes with a lot of blood, guts, poop, and miscellaneous fluids. As a matter of fact, all of life comes with that, too. I'm not prohibited from showing these things because I use it to inform and educate. I use it in the right context.

In the past, I would steer away from showing the blood and guts. Ultimately, I made the decision to go ahead and show it (whenever it happens on the farm) because I feel it's the right thing to do. My mission is to show real life on a dairy farm; the good, the bad, and the ugly. I don't like that our society has been so far removed from the reality of actual farming.

Somewhere along the way, the idea of dairy farming has been sanitized and sugarcoated. Everything I do out here is supposed to be picturesque and pretty. Cows talk as they frolic daintily on rolling green pastures, and occasionally they burst into song. The very second you step on my farm, you are instantly in a Disney princess film.

All joking aside, the problem lies with those who take the reality out of context. An "activist" video comes out, showing only selected images from the whole and sensationalizing what they see as cruelty, gore, and violence.This kind of imagery is too emotionally jarring to

17

people who insist I live in a world of cartoon sunshine and rainbows (there's that phrase again–I kind of like it).

I want people to know that we farmers deal with the realities of life and death every single day on the farm. With over 500 cows to manage, some are born, some will get injured, and some will die. We have sickness, predators, weather events, and infrastructure that can go sideways at a moment's notice. And that's the reality of it all.

Contrary to popular belief, cows do not live forever. They will get sick and they will get old. We do our best to extend their life as well as we can by monitoring their diet, maintaining their medical care, providing ample shelter, water, and food—but cows die. Heck, once in awhile a cow will die and we can't figure out why. I hate that. But, should people be outraged that we have dead cows on the farm? That seems crazy to me. But it sure happens.

Plus, it's not a completely sweet and gentle world. I am occasionally shoulder-deep in a cow's vagina, trying to birth a calf that is having a hard time navigating the birth canal. Incidentally, this happens weekly on our farm. Calving is a difficult and dangerous process. And the calf doesn't always live.

Honestly, we experience death in one form or another every week or ten days around here. Sometimes a calf dies while we're trying to save its life. If a cow does something stupid and breaks a leg, she has to get put down. I may have to shoot the occasional coyote just to protect my herd.

For a segment of the population, I am the bad guy. But if they ever stood in my boots and did my job, they would end up in exactly the same spot, doing exactly the same things.

***

Learning what I could about the inner workings of social media helped me formulate and execute a game plan to give my videos the widest audience possible. For the most part, it worked very well. Most people were very receptive and enjoyed my posts. A lot of people found my videos because they were drawn to a nostalgia within them. What I showed in my clips brought back memories. I received a lot of feedback from folks who had moved closer to cities. My videos brought them back to their childhood when they would spend time with their grandparents on a family farm.

There's an old saying that most people are four generations removed from the farm. In other words, city-dwellers can trace their roots back to when one or both sets of grandparents, great-grandparents, or great-great-grandparents worked the land. When Henry Ford invented the assembly line, our world was ushered into an industrial age. Subsequently, the growth of urban centers really exploded. Before then, most people either grew, raised, trapped, gathered, or shot their food.

I like to flip that saying around. I believe that most farmers are four generations removed from the city. The days of widespread small farms are behind us. More and more, the children of farmers are deciding to leave the industry and move on to working in other career paths. Farming is hard. It requires you to work every day, rain or shine, hot or cold. You're up early, working with your hands, mind, and body. If you have children, you are probably getting to bed late each night, meaning you're constantly trying to catch up on your sleep. There are constant crises you must deal with (a tractor breaks down, for example). And perhaps most importantly nowadays, it's hard to make a living. You need a strong business sense, but also have to be ready for financial ups and downs. There is no company health insurance, your boss doesn't match your 401k contributions, and you don't get paid sick leave or holidays.

I'll go through the economics and day-to-day in later chapters of this book. The point is, farming as an independent practice is dying on the vine. Bigger corporate farms are taking over; therefore, within four generations we may not have small, shade-tree farms anymore.

As we stand today, many people can still recall visiting a family farm. And those people helped seed the growth of my social media vlogs.

From my perspective, the nostalgic sense people get when they see my videos has a reciprocal effect on me. I know that most folks can no longer relate 100% with what I do for a living. They have a conceptual sense of what farmers do, but people basically have a lot to learn. They obviously want to learn. Their desire creates a lot of room for me to help them understand, and that's why I put a lot of time and energy into the videos. There is a lot of information out there, and in my humble opinion, too much of it is complete bullshit. But how would the average reader know? That's why I'm here to separate fact from fiction.

In case you're wondering, I do swear sometimes in real life. Not a whole lot; I was raised to be respectful. I've also had my children around me for most of my adult life. But I'm no stranger to the occasional potty mouth. I don't swear on my videos because I keep them as family-friendly as stark reality can be. When thinking about whether to include an occasional bad word in this book, I decided to pass.

I have a few exceptions. The word "bullshit" feels okay to me. I spend the better part of each day seeing, smelling, and standing in bullshit. Well, technically it's not bullshit. We don't have bulls on the farm. But cow shit seems close enough.

So thank you for tolerating the occasional "b.s." in this book. I really appreciate it.

***

I am writing this book during the summer of 2021. As of now, my TDF Honest Farming Facebook page has just under 600,000 followers. Given that I originated the page in 2017, the growth rate has been astonishing. It's even more astonishing that, for the first year, I only grew to about 20,000 followers.

Okay. I say "only 20,000." Man, I remember feeling like I was top of the world when I hit the 20,000 mark. That blew the top off any number I thought I could achieve. Most dairy influencers hit between 3,000 and 8,000 followers, so 20,000 put me in rarified air. In my sphere, I considered myself to be pretty well-known on Facebook.

At that time, the absolute largest Facebook dairy advocate had roughly 42,000 followers. There was also a smattering of others who had grown to roughly that same size. Some of the bigger accounts, like the 42,000-follwer influencer, were run by people who were less than friendly to me when I reached out to them for advice. Not that any exchange was ugly, but they basically refused to help me. In my opinion, it felt like they didn't want the competition. I honestly don't know what made them to turn away when I reached out, but I wish them well nonetheless. Yet, it still left me with a bad taste in my mouth.

I don't generally like to be around "teeter-totter people." Those are people who think that support is a zero-sum game: if they lift you up, they are then diminished or lowered. I prefer people who think that a rising tide lifts all ships. When you prosper, we all benefit.

When somebody puts out good content, I like to share their stuff. I want to give their exposure a boost. If somebody has a question about how to do what I do, I typically take a few minutes and answer them. Some falls through the cracks because I do get pretty busy, but I would never discourage an honest person who is trying to better themselves and the world around them.

I didn't give up. I turned to other Facebook influencers for advice. One person I like is The Farmer's Wifee, up in Washington State. She chose to misspell her moniker because "The Farmer's Wife" was already taken. She advised me to keep churning out content to improve my presence. The more you put up, the more Facebook users will see you.

She gave me a bunch of pointers over time, and for that I will always be grateful. And while most of her ideas helped me, some weren't really my thing. Everyone is different. What I liked most was that she was community-minded, and not self-centered, when we interacted. I've met her in real life at dairy functions here and there, and she's been great. She is such a wonderful person and so supportive of other people.

I'll give a big shout out to another Facebook friend who has always been nice to me and remains a consistently good person. His moniker is Farmer Tim, and he resides in Canada. I've always had a ton of respect and appreciation for Farmer Tim. He has been available and helpful whenever I had questions about growing my social media presence or when I needed to vent about some of the troglodytes online.

In the agricultural community, we are constantly urging each other to get out of our comfort zone. Talking to other farmers is nice, but we need to get our message out to the broader, non-farmer community. My primary objective is to educate people who aren't dairy farmers. I don't need to tell dairy farmers about what I do every day—they already know. I need to get the word out to school children, urban dwellers, and anyone with curiosity online. I have a lot of respect for The Farmer's Wifee and Farmer Tim (and Modern Day Farm Wife, too) because they also have that mindset.

I hate when people are lied to. I therefore align myself with other folks who work to dispel misinformation. We do our best to jar the thoughts and beliefs of those people who've seen the propaganda from the animal rights frauds. When we show them information that's counter to the beliefs they hold, it challenges them to stop, think, and mentally balance this new information with what they've already seen.

It can be very difficult to change a belief; it requires effort. A message repeated over and over has a lot of staying power, whether it's something you tell yourself internally or something you hear externally. It is the strongest tool we use to learn, and it helps cement that information into our memory. Thus, when someone tries to learn something new that contradicts what's cemented into memory, it takes even more repetition of the new information to override the old information. And that is not easy!

As I mentioned before, Facebook's news feed algorithm will show a user content that it thinks they will engage with by looking at what they've already engaged with. Thus, there's a good chance that they'll see the same things (which may contain misinformation) over and over again, working its way into their mind. Those posts may look a little different at first, but the message is always the same. And that same message continues to re-affirm the misinformation they may have already learned.

This is what I'm up against.

But I don't give up. I engage with readers. I post fun and relevant videos. I post at the best times. I use all the right keywords and hashtags. I do all I can to improve my social media reach. I generate content that a consumer can understand and weigh against other viewpoints they've seen. It takes time and patience. But I've got both.

***

Moving through 2018, my 20,000 follower number continued to rise. I wish I could say there was a moment of astronomical lift-off, but the growth curve remained pretty steady. I continued to grind away, and my follower count continued to gradually accumulate.

I discovered that the more followers I received, the easier it was to get more. Hypothetically, if each follower shares a video I post, it could be seen by other people who weren't aware of me. For example, if one person shared a video and ten of their followers saw it, that's potentially ten new followers. If that person had 100 followers, that meant a video could be seen by roughly 1,000 new people. If that person had 1,000 followers, that meant each video could be seen by roughly 10,000 new people, and so on.

By and large, the growth was 100% organic. I tried to promote posts through the Facebook ad system a few times, but was disappointed by the results. The ad system works great for some folks, but for me it became a complete waste of money. I would spend twenty dollars to to promote a post and I would get about 300 extra views. Put that 300 against the 10,000 views the post normally got without paid promotion, the benefit was dwarfed by the cost. For folks with smaller accounts on Facebook, paying twenty dollars for 300 new viewers might be a good investment. For me, my 10,000 viewers would share my videos to more than 300 new viewers on their own. It seemed like my account had reached some sort of critical mass. It was growing by leaps and bounds all on its own.

I uploaded content daily. If something interesting happened on the farm, I put up a video about it. Good or bad, I put the "social" in social media and it worked. Most folks might post a few times per week; I posted a few times per day. The more I posted, the more people responded. It was a whirlwind of work, but it was also energizing. Several times over the past couple years, I have been staggered by the numbers on my Facebook page's reach.

I do my best to not lose perspective or grow too big for my britches. But once in awhile, I am reminded of how much I have accomplished and how important it is to treat my status as an honor, and not a justification for hubris.

But I still get happy about my accomplishments. Let me share a letter that I recently received from Mallory Phelan, Executive Director of Oregon Aglink. This letter followed the organization's announcement that I had won the 2021 Oregon Ag Connection Award. It honored me for the outreach and education I was doing to advocate for dairy farmers. I reposted the award announcement, along with a couple of my thoughts about it. Molly was tagged in to my repost, so all of the notifications of people reacting to my repost were also sent to her account.

Derrick:
This is unreal. A little glimpse into what your
notifications for comments and shares is like on

the daily. It's one thing to look through your posts
as someone who follows your page and sees the
comments, shares, and likes. But it's a whole other
thing to get the notifications of people's support for
you, and how you've impacted their understanding
of cows and the dairy industry. I know I'm going to
say this more than once this year, but thank you for
everything you do in sharing your life online. You
humanize agriculture for people unlike anyone else
in Oregon. It's inspiring, and I'm so thankful for the
work and time you give to make it happen.
~Mallory

I guess I should have told her to turn off her notifications when I tagged her in, but it was cool to be reminded that what I do is both good and important. I'm in it every day, so don't oftenrealize how much of an inspiration I could be. I learned long ago to turn my notification bell off. Most times, I don't see all the comments any more. It would take me all day to keep up with them, and I've got just too many chores to do.

Honestly, the good folks who follow my page are fairly active as a community in and of themselves. As a result, my notifications have been off the charts since I passed that coveted 20,000 follower mark. But it didn't stop there.The growth was steady through 2017 and 2018 until I reached 100,000 followers. I reached that benchmark in 2019, and from there the curve grew sharper and steeper.

With God as my witness, I don't know exactly what spurred the jump. I didn't make an appearance on The Daily podcast, I wasn't featured on the front page of the Wall Street Journal, and I didn't invent a cost-effective way to desalinate sea water. What I did do, however, was move outside of the agricultural bubble.

The 100,000 mark probably topped off the number of farmers, agricultural industry folks, and farm families/extended circles around the country—and probably in many English-speaking countries around the world. Once I broke free of that finite group, the growth of my account spiked because the potential audience spiked as well.

If I look at the top cities these days where people interact the most with my posts, they are parallel to the most populated cities in the United States. My top cities are Los Angeles, New York, Chicago, a couple cities in Texas, and the two urban centers close to me, Portland and Seattle. To consider that the residents of these urban centers are interested in what I do on the farm is a testimony to how well my mission has been working. My reach has captured the curiosity of hundreds of thousands of folks who do not have farming backgrounds. And that is exactly why I do these videos.

As of the writing of this book, my Facebook account sits somewhere between 550,000 and 600,000 followers. I'm not fanatical enough to track it every single day, but that's not to say I don't pay attention to the numbers. I wish I could be completely punk rock and say I don't care about the numbers. But in order to understand the ever-changing state of social media and continue to extend the reach of my messaging, I do have to keep up with what works and what does not. That understanding requires that I watch the figures. The numbers ebb and flow with how well each platform, especially Facebook, distributes my videos.

Still, the numbers astound me. When my Facebook page reach surpassed the 50,000,000 mark, meaning over fifty million people see something on my page each month, I had to put down my cup of coffee for a moment and stare at my phone in disbelief. By the time you read these words, and barring anything unforeseen, that number will be even higher.

Not bad for a farm kid who stands in cow shit all day.

Most of my posts reach 100-200,000 people. They each get shared thousands of times, so the audience grows likewise. The best video I've ever posted (with regard to numbers) was a raw video of a tough calving. That one reached over 100 million people, as of this writing.

I had to turn off the comments to that video. I got tired of people telling me I was doing everything all wrong. Everyone is an expert when they are sitting in the audience and not actually in the ring. I'm reminded of a famous quote from Theodore Roosevelt. He included this passage within a longer speech delivered to the Sorbonne (Paris) in April of 1910, but the sentiment rings timelessly true:

"It is not the critic who counts; not the man who points out how the strong man stumbles, or where the doer of deeds could have done them better. The credit belongs to the man who is actually in the arena, whose face is marred by dust and sweat and blood; who strives valiantly; who errs, who comes short again and again, because there is no effort without error and shortcoming; but who does actually strive to do the deeds; who knows great enthusiasms, the great devotions; who spends himself in a worthy cause; who at the best knows in the end the triumph of high achievement, and who at the worst, if he fails, at least fails while daring greatly, so that his place shall never be with those cold and timid souls who neither know victory nor defeat."

As for other social media platforms, I do not have a Tik-Tok account. I'm concerned that their parent company is in China, whose government is real big on censorship. Also, I just don't vibe with their overall style. They were formed after I already had a successful account on a different platform. I don't have the time to make video stories that are specific to their app, and I don't feel any need to join yet another video-based platform.

Likewise, I don't pay much attention to Twitter. I have an account, but I mostly retweet posts from friends. I'm only on Twitter once or twice per week. In my experience, Twitter is the worst platform with regard to bots and internet tough guys, so it has been more a waste of my time and energy than a benefit to my overall mission statement.

Instagram is the only other platform I pay attention to. Unlike Facebook, where I am mindful to analyze growth patterns and manage my followers, I watch Instagram for a different reason. I have been testing it to see if, when, how, and why Instagram shadowbans. I am insanely curious to see exactly what I can and cannot talk about on their platform. I want to know what happens with a shadowban.

For those of you not familiar with the term, "shadowbanning" is the practice of suppressing viewership a user's content from an online community without the knowledge of the user. The content isn't outright deleted; that would be Orwellian if your post doesn't flagrantly violate community guidelines. Instead, the post is allowed to remain visible, but the number of people who can see it is severely limited. It's subtle, but it allows the platform to control content without technically censoring it.

The original intention of shadowbanning was to keep away the trolls. No one will see the nasty comments or the spam except for the person who posts it. The views on the post drop, thus the troll thinks everyone is ignoring them. They get discouraged with the platform and move on to another site (Thompson, 2009). Of course, like any well-intentioned idea, the platforms that implemented it started abusing it. Instagram has become infamous for shadowbanning, although they continually deny it; they won't even use the word "shadowban." But it sure seems they have done a lot of apologizing for stifled content (Thomas, 2021).

So, I gave Instagram a try. I don't really need to present you with a list of grievances. Let's just say that it's been an interesting journey.

The standout example of my Instagram experiences happened when I got a formal warning from Instagram. I made a video with my daughter, Reagan when she was just two years old. She and I had been playing in the mud and were covered from head to toe. It was silly fun and a relatively tame video, showing a side of parenting that I'm sure every mom and dad has experienced.

Instagram didn't have a problem with the mud or the parenting; they had a problem with Reagan's attire. Her shirt was off, showing her two-year-old torso. I got notified for posting child pornography.

Listen, I get it. I don't personally understand how anyone could get off looking at a two year old, but I'm not naïve. I know that very creepy and very damaged predators are out there. Therefore, I understand that Instagram has to monitor those issues as conservatively as they can.

So I received a message about my community standards violation.

Fine. I won't do that again.

In the aftermath, an odd thing happened: my account was severely restricted. For roughly three months following that incident, my posts—on an account with approximately 50,000 followers—were seen by about 500 people each time. That was a sharp decline from my usual numbers. This made absolutely no sense to me.

I contested their verdict that labeled the video as child pornography. My appeal essentially went nowhere.

Lesson learned.

All in all, social media has helped to spread the word. My presence has been good for my personal farm, obviously, but I am more proud of how it has brought Tillamook dairy products to the attention of new consumers all over the country. I am most proud of how my presence has educated and entertained people who have never been to a farm, but are curious to know what we farmers do to keep the world fed in a hard-working and ethical way.

Chapter 2
Dairy Is Scary and So Is Life

It was an activist video that got me started on this journey. But, *Dairy is Scary* is only one member of the Holy Trinity of Shock Videos. The other two "shock-umentaries" are *What the Health* (2017) and *Dominion* (2018). All three have been debunked by a variety of highly qualified veterinarians, scientists, and farmers.

As I have mentioned, online misinformation is the main weapon of choice for animal rights activists.The main issues distorted by all these "documentaries" are: down cows (also known as "downers"), animal welfare, cow/calf separation, and artificial insemination.

The strategy of these films, as is the strategy of all propaganda, is to make dairy farmers out to be frauds and murderers. They take the standard practices of a dairy farm and manipulate the narrative to create a strong, irrational, and emotional impact on viewers who are unaware of the actuality of dairy farming.

That's the key element here: these are folks who honestly don't know any better.

The reason I am writing this book (and, I hope, you are reading it) is to help everyone know better. There's no sense getting pulled into an emotional hailstorm if the information you are reacting to is completely false. The practices followed on dairy farms all over the country are in place for the good of the animals.

To help you, the reader, know better, I will analyze, critique, and debunk the short film *Dairy Is Scary*. Get comfortable, and get ready for some dairy reality.

***

Down Cows and Animal Welfare

Referred to as "downers" in the video, down cows are, quite literally, cows that are lying down and cannot (or will not) get up. The video shows a down cow, plays up how sad the situation is for the cow, and then implies that the farmer coldly and dismissively "gets rid of the cow," the inference being that the cow is subsequently slaughtered for meat.

I'll go on record to say that this is completely false. A downed cow is a very serious situation for farmers, and this video portrayed it in the worst possible light.

There are a number of reasons cows might be on the ground and unable to lift themselves to their feet. It could be something as simple as milk fever (parturient paresis), a bad case of mastitis, or something more daunting, like a serious injury. Most farmers can pretty quickly distinguish which of the basic ailments might lead to a downed cow.

Milk fever was given its name because the cow is probably hot to the touch; hence, the "fever." Or, on more rare occasions, milk fever may make the cow feel deathly cold. But they'll always have "the wobbles." The cow will have difficulty standing on her own without wobbling and shaking so hard, she falls back down to the ground.

What causes milk fever is a lack of calcium. The cow's body is already depleted of calcium through the calving process; when their milk comes in, it robs even more precious calcium from her body. For cows that were already on the border of calcium deficiency, this creates the milk fever condition.

Usually, a simple fix takes care of the situation. We give the cow calcium, and she recovers quickly. The recovery rate from milk fever is quite good, even in its advanced stages. Without treatment, the death rate from milk fever is about 75% of those afflicted (Allen, 2015). We actually save the cow from dying rather than take the cow to die. The activist messaging is a lie.

The incidence of milk fever can be mitigated with preventative measures. I believe the old adage is, "An ounce of prevention is worth a pound of cure." Farmers are all about prevention. What could be a better use of your time than heading off problems before they can begin?

In this case, we give a bolus (a big pill) to every cow after they have a calf. The bolus contains calcium, magnesium and phosphorous. It's nothing more than a fresh cow vitamin pack. If we have a cow with a history of difficult calcium regulation, we may administer a bolus before she has the calf, and then a couple more after calving. Better to be safe than sorry.

Mastitis, a bacterial infection of the udder, has its own challenges and requires more care. At a glance, the cow will have sunken eyes and go from wanting to give milk to not wanting to do much at all. A quick check of the cow's hindquarters will reveal swelling and redness in the udder. You can tell the cow is in significant discomfort, as any human woman who has contracted mastitis while breastfeeding will tell you.

The disease is caused by a number of bacterial strains that get into the udder. Transmission can be through bacteria on the milking machine or through nursing, as calves may have the dormant bacteria in their mouth.

No one single bacterium can cause mastitis and therefore, treatment has to be somewhat tailored to the cause. Penicillin is probably the most common antibiotic treatment, although certain bacteria respond better to certain antibiotics. Tests help match cause to cure. Of course, our veterinarian will always make the final call on the best course of treatment.

One surprising issue vilified in the video is that while a cow is being treated with antibiotics, their milk cannot be mixed with the milk going to market. The treated cow will still have to be milked, but her milk gets dumped. This isn't a villainous practice because the antibiotics will find their way into the cow's milk, which then contaminates the milk for human consumption.

Sticking with the "Ounce of Prevention" model, we do all we can to minimize the risk of mastitis in our herd. We sterilize the milking machines after each use, we keep the barn areas clean and free of things that can carry bacteria, and we manage the health of the calves. Unfortunately, just like in the human environment, we cannot completely eliminate bacteria in the world around the cows. They get sick once in awhile. And, just like in the human environment, we don't just kill a sick cow. We treat the cow and get her healthy again. Then she returns to life as a productive member of the herd.

Cows and people will get sick, recover, and move ahead with life.

It makes absolutely no sense to kill a cow in these instances. Think about it in strict financial terms. It is true that the milk of a sick cow cannot be sold by the farmer. That's smart. But which do you think is more of a financial burden: treating the cow with a bolus or round of antibiotics, or purchasing and raising a new cow who is about two years off from producing milk?

It doesn't take a math whiz to solve that riddle.

Here's another interesting fact that the video fails to mention. It is illegal to send a cow to slaughter if she cannot walk. It's a law that passed in 2006 called The BSE Ongoing Surveillance Program. This was done to prevent the spread of mad cow disease, or Bovine Spongiform Encephalitis. Cattle have to be able to walk under their own power into the slaughter facility to show they don't have BSE, according to the U.S. Department of Agriculture's Animal and Plant Health Inspection Service (2020).

In the end, the farmer will do all he or she can do to get the cow healthy again. Only after all treatments have been exhausted will the farmer opt to euthanize the cow on the farm. I don't know if I can stress this point enough, but euthanizing a cow is always the last possible resort. I will spend time in Chapter Six talking about end-of-life issues with cows. But, this is not a pleasant part of farming. Unless a farmer has disturbing mental issues (as with any profession, they do exist), this is a necessary, but extremely difficult act, to complete.

As for me, I hate it. I really hate it. I get it, but hate it.

Again, the goal is to take a sick cow, get her healthy, and make her a productive member of the farm society again. Make no mistake about it; every farm is its own society. The farmer is in charge, so the society isn't a democracy. But the health and well-being of the cows is the primary force guiding the decisions made by their benevolent monarch.

We have a high batting average when it comes to curing illnesses in our cows because our protocols have been honed over centuries of dairy farming. My staff and I work closely with our veterinarians to implement those protocols. By "protocols," I mean that I have an entire binder of rules, processes, and guidelines that I am required to keep and adhere to when it comes to handling sick cows. It also extends beyond illness. We have procedures in place to deal with pretty much any situation you can think of with cows.

The binder is a requirement for me because I'm a member of the Farmers Assuring Responsible Management (FARM) program. The program was created in 2009 by the National Milk Producers Federation, who created guidelines for responsible dairy farm management. Through the program, farms are certified in three areas: animal care, environmental stewardship, and antibiotic stewardship.

We take our role as custodians of our animals, our land and facilities, and the responsible use of antibiotics very seriously. FARM is an industry-led program—it isn't mandated by law. It's an organization formed by dairy farmers to make sure dairy farming moves ahead in the most responsible way possible. We're a proactive bunch; we certainly don't need the government to tell us to be good people.

For those who may be skeptical, I'd like you to think in terms of common sense. In order to be successful, doing the right thing is going to be more profitable for the farm in the long run. Using ethical business practices builds consumer loyalty (which generates more consumer money), it enhances the business' reputation, and it helps avoid costly legal problems. Doing the right thing makes good financial sense.

Yes, we could just discard sick cows. But to what end? Replacing cows is far more costly than caring for cows.

Yes, we can abuse our animals. But to what end? Stressed-out cows produce less milk, which means less profit for the farmer.

Yes, we can try to sneak bad milk in with the good. But to what end? Our industry, like all food, is strictly regulated by the FDA. We would get fined and eventually dropped, which would put us out of business.

Yes, we could save time and money by not sterilizing our milking machines or not keeping the barns clean. But to what end? Now we have to spend more money on sick cows that don't produce sellable milk, and…well, you get the point.

The most profitable companies take care of their employees and their customers. No smart businessman would destroy their profit base. Healthy cows give better milk.

Thus, a farmer would prefer to not have down cows. From a business and personal standpoint, they take a lot of time to deal with. If I have a down cow on my farm, that one sick cow might take 30 to 60 minutes of my time to tend to her. My day isn't packed every single minute, but an hour spent with one cow will throw off my routine.

That's why we do so much work toward prevention. In fact, we rarely have down cows on the farm. We work closely with a nutritionist to make sure the cows are getting all they need in their feed. We work with the veterinarian to conduct regular herd health checks.

I mix their food to keep it right. We keep the water troughs clean. Everything we do is geared toward keeping cows healthy. Using our time to manage 500 cows is more efficient than using it to manage one individual cow at a time.

We have ten employees on the farm. There are four family members (my mom and dad, my wife, and myself), and six employees from the community. That means that the profits from our farm have to support eight families (mine, my parents, and the families of each of the six external employees). We want to be profitable to make the lives of everyone on the farm better. That means making sure the lives of our cows are safe, clean, and relaxed.

If you go to a dairy farm, the routine will seem fairly basic. You probably wouldn't realize that the farmer's actions are guided by a set of formal protocols. To be honest, most of what we do is fairly basic. Cows, like any animal, are creatures of habit and routine. On days when nothing goes wrong, the farmers and cows do their thing and, for the most part, it's a smooth flow of action.

However, the higher the cow population, the higher the chance that something will go sideways somewhere. These are the times in particular that the farmer and the farm staff need to know what to do, so as to not make it worse. That's where the protocols come into play. We prepare ourselves for the "what ifs" that pop up when you least expect them.

***

Cow/Calf Separation

This issue in the video was particularly troubling to me. The producer encouraged viewers to assign human emotions to cows, which is known as anthropomorphism. Anthropomorphism is a normal human behavior; the areas of our brain that trigger empathy and understanding also light up when we anthropomorphize (Nauert, 2018). However, animal rights extremists use a form of toxic anthropomorphism where the imagery flashes into view so fast, the person watching only has time to feel emotions instead of critically think. This is most evident when very fast jump cuts are shown (out of context) of wailing cows and calves. Because we are human, we anthropomorphize; we interpret the sounds of these animals as to be cries of distress (Brown & McLean, 2013). Parents (yes, even dads) deeply empathize with this interpretation. No one wants to think about forcibly taking a baby from its momma.

Dairy cattle, however, are different from human beings.

To illustrate my point, I need to differentiate beef cows and dairy cows. To the uninitiated, a cow is a cow. But generations upon generations of breeding has honed the different breeds into the best version of what they do, be it beef cattle or dairy cows. Holstein, Jersey, and Guernsey are common dairy breeds. Angus, Hereford, Wagyu, and Longhorns are common beef breeds. Like all mammals, every breed of cow will produce milk for their young. And, like every breed of cow, they can all be eaten as beef. However, each breed has been bred to get the best milk (Jersey) or the best beef (Wagyu).

The life of today's beef cow closely resembles the lives of beef cattle eons ago. They live their lives outdoors, spending the majority of their time on a range. They are more muscular—beefy, if you will—and can survive the long trek of a cattle drive (which still happen in today's world). However, the rancher will still work hard to keep the herd as stress-free as possible. Their goal is to raise big, healthy cows.

Breeding on beef farms has started moving toward artificial insemination these days, but most of it is still done naturally. A bull is released into the herd and nature takes its course. Beef cows are a heartier bunch, and their bodies are better equipped to handle the concussion of the mating process. Make no mistake; a bull is forceful while he's getting the job done.

When beef cows calve, it can be unsupervised and it happens out on the range most of the time. With beef cows, maternal instinct is huge. Calving on the range means that the cow has to protect her calf from predators, the elements, and other cows. Survival of the calf depends upon the mother's protection.

However, the life of a dairy cow is a life of leisure.

Dairy cattle have been coddled for many generations. In all honesty, a maternal bond with her calf is no longer necessary—and hasn't been for a long, long time. When they give birth, the calves are taken to special pens where they are looked after and very well protected by the farm staff. They are health-checked by our veterinarian and given medical attention if necessary. They are sheltered from the elements, kept fortified against predators, and sequestered from other, larger cows.

Survival of the calf is pretty much guaranteed without the cow needing a fierce maternal instinct.

Since the first known dairy farmers of Anatolia in 7000 BC, cows have been selectively bred to avoid any kind of ferocity (Hirst, 2019). I honestly don't know for certain, but I'm confident that even back then, dairy farmers would prefer that a cow not try to kill them when they attempted to remove the calf. So cows that were more aggressive were removed from the farm, and cows that were more passive were allowed to stay. Aggressive dairy cows were most likely killed for food, and passive cows most likely bred. Taking a page out of Gregor Mendel's genetic playbook, passivity has become the dominant trait among dairy cows, and that fierce maternal instinct has become a rare recessive trait. Granted, I'm not a professor of bovine history. These decisions and trends began long before a Josi set foot in Oregon. What I do know through actual experience on a farm with over 500 cows is that they just don't have it in them to fret when a calf is taken away after birth.

Keep this in mind: if you have a cute puppy or kitten or foal, that animal had to be separated from its mother at some point. You may not have been there to see it. Yet, for anyone who has brought home a new puppy, you have witnessed first-hand the trauma of that separation. The pup will likely cry for most of the first few nights as they acclimate to their new home environment, away from their brothers and sisters and mother.

Animals bred as pets will remain with their mother through the nursing period. Calves will be separated from their mothers within the first few hours following birth. There is a quantifiable difference among the different types of animals when it comes to time spent with the mother, but studies have shown that it's actually easier for the cow if the calf is separated shortly after birth (Mikus, Marzel, and Mikus, 2020; Stehulová, Lidfors, and Spinka, 2007; Weary and Chua, 2000).

Nature can be brutal. In the wild, that calf would end up separating from its mother when the next calving period rolls around. To protect the prospective new calf from its older, larger sibling, the mother would kick the living crap out of the 500-pound yearling calf to get it away from both her and her newborn.

Sometimes in my social media, I'll get a similar comment to this: "I was raised next to a farm, and I could hear the poor mothers bellowing when their baby was taken from them."

I'll always ask if the commenter lived near a beef farm or a dairy farm. Invariably, the answer is a beef farm. What the commenter was hearing from the beef farm was the weaning period, where the calf is separated from its mother. The distressing sounds the mother is making has more to do with physical discomfort from her milk drying up; this is known as "dry-off." Human mothers go through the same pain when they stop breastfeeding, too. The calves will also bellow because they want that familiar font of food. I repeat: it's the milk, not the mother cow, the calf wants. Once they get fed with their new food, they're quiet and content.

I have gone out of my way to make several videos showing how we separate a calf from its mother. The intent is to show the viewer that the mother cow sees me take the calf, and then goes about her day. She strolls off, grazing and resuming her normal activities. I will peruse the comments after posting such a video, and invariably, a number of people will say things like, "Poor cow. She misses her calf."

What? You just watched a video of me taking the calf, putting it in the calf pen, and then back the cow, who is eating some food. She's as chill as can be. Yet, somehow, this viewer thinks that the cow is distressed. Please excuse me if I don't repeat myself about the dangers of attributing your feelings to the cow. Not even scientists do this!

Other people are bound and determined to think I am up to no good. They ignore what their eyes see right in front of them. Their comments are along the lines of: "That's not really her calf. You staged the whole thing and switched cows to make it look like the mamma didn't care."

Again…*what?* Have any of the hundreds of videos I've posted over the years ever given any indication that I am trying to dupe the world? As I have said several times, to what end? What kind of result would I want from trying to lie? There is nothing in it for me to choreograph an elaborate ruse like that. I show reality on reality's terms. That is what I do!

Among dairy cows, the mother is not invested in any bond with her baby. Once that calf is out of sight, the mother has forgotten about it. Almost immediately, the mother is standing up (unless she's not feeling well), eating and drinking some water. These mothers move forward and take care of their own needs.

At the risk of sounding arrogant, I'll restate a point I made earlier. Following the birth, I am able to take better care of that calf than the mother. We have strict protocols in place to maintain optimal health of all the animals involved.

For example, we "dip" the navel. Just as with human newborns, one of the most susceptible areas on a calf is its navel, so we work hard to protect that area. The umbilical cord is a wick that connects the now-ejected cow's placenta to the calf's abdomen and into its stomach cavity. We make sure it is clean, sanitized, and carefully clipped. That way, bad bacteria can't crawl up into the umbilical cord and into the newborn.

We also test the colostrum. Colostrum is a special breast milk produced by mammals (including humans) before regular breast milk is released. We test it for the correct protein levels and to ensure it's of high quality before we give it the calf. We also ensure the calf gets the colostrum in a timely manner. The passive transfer of immunities through the colostrum is a major deciding factor in helping the calf lead a healthy, productive life. We keep the cows as well-protected from disease as we can, but their natural immunities are their best defense against environmental diseases that could threaten their well-being.

Last, we monitor the calf's eating. We make sure they are fed enough and that they are receiving all the nutrients they need to grow.

***

Artificial Insemination

To make sure we have the resources necessary to take care of the calves at the highest level, we control the number and the frequency of calves being born. Every cow calves, so we rotate their birthing cycles so there is a steady and largely predictable flow of calves. The means through which we do this is artificial insemination.

"Activist" videos imply that this is an unnatural process, and therefore harmful to the cows. In Chapter Three, I have a comprehensive discussion on Artificial Insemination (AI) and calving. But here, I'd like to address a few issues from the video that touch on artificial insemination.

We calve year-round on the farm. The young cows are called heifers until they give birth themselves. Cows will naturally birth once per year; their estrus cycle is set up for that timeline. They reach their first estrus at roughly one year of age, at which point they begin to draw the attention of the bulls. Hence, they would 'naturally' have their first calf at age 18 months. On our farm, we actually wait until the heifer is two years old before she has her first calf.

This waiting period is put in place for the well-being of the heifers—to let them have more time to grow and develop. When they are bigger and stronger, they are better equipped to manage the physical strain of pregnancy. This provides them with a better recovery and survival rate.

Compare this to human beings. A girl could become pregnant when she hits menarche, her first period. By age eleven or twelve, her body has the hormonal and physical structures to become pregnant and carry a fetus until delivery. But she is young and still growing. Her body would be forced to split resources between building her own body and building the baby in her womb. Therefore, her chances of complications are higher than if she waits until she is 18, 21, or 25 to have her first baby.

We understand this and follow the same chain of logic on the farm. Beginning at age two, we artificially inseminate the cow once per year. This is the natural cycle in all cows, since they will give birth annually during their peak reproductive years. As with all species, their lives and

35

cycles are designed to produce young at the most optimal times. It's all about survival.

In fact, they will probably be calving every ten or eleven months. As soon as they hit their first heat following delivery, the bull will notice. If their mating is successful, the gestational cycle will begin again. Technically, this is how their estrus cycle is set up. A cow will show her first heat cycle about thirty days after calving. A cow's gestation period is 274 days, compared to 280 days for a human. You can do the math from there.

In a natural setting, the bull doesn't care about the health or well-being of the cow. He has one thing on his mind, and he's going to mate while he can. Therefore, the cows could be impregnated immediately as soon as the bull detects they're in heat.

On a farm, we allow more recovery time to maximize the health of the mother and the calf. We have a mandatory wait time of 60 days (90 for some cows, based upon their health) before we will even consider breeding her again.

It's not a perfect science, but we are pretty good at making sure the cows have a safe time table for giving birth, fully recovering, and then entering heat and giving birth again. A variety of factors can affect the reproductive cycle.

The temperature of the environment is a factor that has an effect on a cow's estrus cycle. She may not go into heat that cycle, and we will have to wait another 21 days before she is in heat again. We recently had a bad day of heat in the Tillamook Valley. The high temperature went from 70 degrees Fahrenheit (21.1 degrees Celsius) one day to 103 degrees Fahrenheit (39.4 Celsius) the next. The following day, the temperature went back to normal.

That spike in temperature was astonishingly traumatic for the cows, which have no real means to escape or dissipate the heat. We did all we could to keep them cool; we hosed them down, created better air flow in the barn, and made sure drinking water was constantly available. Cows drink about 40 gallons of fresh water per day and up to 80 gallons on hot days. But it's near impossible to outsmart nature.

I take my hat off to the staff of the farm on that day. We lost one cow out of 500. It hurt me inside to lose that cow. I walked away wondering if I did enough or if I could have done something differently to save her. To make matters worse, we thought we had saved her. She had recovered and was interested in eating that evening. Seemingly out of nowhere, she passed away later that night. It was an awful feeling. However, it could have been worse. The staff rallied and saved the lives of many cows that day. I'm so proud of them.

For the most part, a cow's cycle is as predictable as a human woman's cycle. And, as with human women, a cow's cycle can be affected by environmental factors. Nutrition and stress can throw off a menstrual cycle. We control these factors the best we can on the farm to keep the cows as stress free and as regular as possible. This helps us keep an even number of cows birthing year-round. That way, we are not overwhelmed with an influx of calves, making it easier to manage their health.

After all, healthy cows are productive cows.

Chapter 3
Artificial Insemination

As a practice in modern farming, artificial insemination is a relatively new phenomenon. In the United States, artificial insemination got its start in the late 1930s. An AI cooperative formed in New Jersey in 1938, motiving others to start up in Minnesota, New York, Wisconsin, and other states across the nation (Foote, 2002).

I do remember our family having a "clean up bull" on the farm. A clean up bull is kept to breed cows that have difficulty getting pregnant artificially. In other words, we use the bull if science can't make a viable embryo germinate and implant in the uterine wall. The bull will do it the old fashioned way, which tends to work more often than not.

Why not just breed the cows the old fashioned way all the time? Why bother with all the AI stuff if we have a perfectly virile bull running around who can get cows pregnant?

If you're asking that question, you've probably never seen a bull mate with a cow. It ain't pretty. I mentioned earlier that bulls are strong and determined beasts. Bulls are interested in impregnating a cow as quickly and efficiently as possible—and frankly, it ends up being quite violent. Mating will take a toll on a healthy, large cow; now, imagine a smaller breed of cow. If the bull is a rampaging, hormone-driven, 2,000-pound bundle of BANG, and the cow is a dainty, 600-pound "innocent" debutant, the odds of the smaller female walking away unscathed are very low.

In Jersey breeds, the bulls are a little smaller, so the chances of a successful mating are much higher. With species like Holsteins and Guernseys, the bulls can be much larger and they'll mate with more brute force.

AI also takes away the possibility of STDs. Just like humans, cows and bulls can get venereal diseases, too. The big three diseases dairy cows catch directly from bulls are Bovine Herpes 1 (BHV), Trichomoniasis, and Vibriosis. The first disease is caused by a virus; the other two are bacterial. But, all three can render a cow infertile and cause her calf to be stillborn (Larkins, 2019).

Thanks to artificial insemination, we don't have these problems on our farm. We are strictly an artificial insemination operation. Thus, there is a 0% risk among our herd.

Once again, healthy cows are productive cows!

As a kid, I also recall the demise of the bulls. It seemed that every bull would eventually reach a point where they were too aggressive for the farmers to handle. At that time, they would be sent down the road to be slaughtered for beef. They simply grew too dangerous to be around. You never knew exactly when it was going to happen, but it always did.

I remember one bull that was in this stage of his career. He had my uncle pinned against a wall and he looked like he was trying to smash into my uncle. My uncle got himself out of the situation (probably with the help of my dad). That was also the day that bull was made into hamburger. He had passed the point of no return.

AI is safer for everyone, human and bovine.

These days, when a bull is raised as a breeder, he lives a life of ease.The bulls on stud farms are called "AI Studs," and are completely pampered. From the perspective of the bull, he's living his best life. Because of artificial insemination, bulls don't even have to go through the calisthenics of intercourse—they are milked for their semen. He spends his days eating, exercising, eliminating, ejaculating, and just existing.

I've never actually seen the process of semen extraction, but know quite a bit about how it is extracted. There are three main practices to the act of extracting semen. One involves sliding an electronic probe into the bull's anus. The probe vibrates, stimulating the prostate into ejaculating. A second involves sliding a bull's penis into a pump that stimulates them until they ejaculate. The third method involves the bull using a "jumper cow." A jumper cow is basically a fake hindquarter of a cow. The bull sees it, mounts it, and then copulates until ejaculation.

The semen is collected and divided into thin vials called "straws," and the vials are sold all over the world. A straw of bull semen looks just like what the name implies—it is a long, thin plastic tube that hold about 0.5 ml of semen. The straws are sealed and frozen at the stud farm, and then transported anywhere around the globe. Some of that frozen bull semen may be in the cargo hold of the next airplane you're on.

So, put that in your straw!

Bull semen can be worth its weight in gold. The demand makes for a strong market, particularly for bulls that carry certain genetic markers for qualities a farmer would want in his or her cattle. A bull may tend to throw cows that produce more milk, have more robust immune systems, live a long life, have an easier time during their own calving process, or all of the above. It used to be that farmers had to rely on instinct and experience to select good bulls for their semen. Rudimentary, manual record-keeping was used, but it wasn't an exact science. In the twenty-first century, genetic mapping and testing has gotten us to the point where scientists can analyze the DNA of a bull and know the specific markers for these qualities.

Now, reproductive technology has gotten us to the point where we can select semen specifically for gender. It's not to the point where it's 100% accurate, but it's pretty close.

From a financial standpoint, the most desirable qualities of a bull can make a huge difference. When you figure that a single ejaculation can net over a thousand straws of semen, the numbers add up quickly. The lifespan of a bull's "fertile zone" is about ten years, from roughly one year of age up until they are ten or twelve years old. Their peak performance lasts about five years, but that can equal a lot of semen.

A single straw of bull semen can run from five to ten dollars USD on the low end. On the high end, for special bulls, especially within the dairy industry, a straw can run you anywhere from fifty to one hundred dollars USD.

We don't climb the ladder all the way to the top with our herd. However, we do take advantage of the top genetic research in the industry when we select and purchase bull semen. We have brought in bull semen from Denmark, Canada, and Australia in the past.

Make no mistake: the bull is important to the process, but the artificial insemination work really begins once he's done his thing and submitted his sample.

***

A cow is in heat for roughly twelve hours. That's not a huge window, but we have it down to a science on the farm. Once you see them act like they're in heat, we wait twelve hours to breed them. If it seems as though we have arrived late to the party, we'll only wait eight hours to breed her. In essence, you want to breed them at the tail end of their heat.

No pun intended.

The way they show estrus isn't exactly subtle, so we pick up on the signs pretty easily. In case you're wondering, a cow will naturally signal a bull that it's "about that time" by going through mounting rituals with other cows.

Most animals signal estrus through scent. Cows are no exception. A bull can smell a cow in heat up to six miles away (Moran & Doyle, 2015). Of course, I have a really big farm, and I'd have to hope that the bull was standing down wind of the cow to pick up her scent.

The process is simple in theory, but takes special training and a lot of repetition to get the feel for how to inseminate a cow. On the farm, me, my dad, and one other employee have taken training courses and are able to conduct the procedure properly and safely. If none of us are available during that short window of late estrus, we can contact a service in town that handles the procedure for us.

It isn't impossible to find AI techs…but it's as difficult as finding veterinarians who work with large animals. They're out there, but they're just not nearly as plentiful as you would like them to be, especially when you're in a bind. The number of large-animal vets is beginning to shrink because the demand is decreasing. Farms are consolidating, with smaller operations selling out to bigger operations. As farms scale up and go corporate, the company will provide their own veterinarian and techs on staff. Once on the payroll of a corporation, those vets and techs are taken out of the general population.

***

Before I give the essentials of dairy cow breeding, I need to bring up an insane point. Animal rights activists sexualize this process. They imply that farmers have a screw loose because they somehow get off by messing with the hindquarter of a cow in estrus. I'm here to tell you, there is NOTHING even REMOTELY appealing about sticking my arm up a cow's ass.

Yeah, I'm serious: this is what some people think.

I don't know of anyone in the industry who gets their jollies from doing that. And I don't want to know anyone like that, either. This is a process that has to be done. Like most unpleasant necessities in life, someone's got to do it. My dad and I run the farm, so we step up to the plate and take one for the team.

Besides, both hands are needed for the procedure.

All joking aside, I am going to be as blunt as descriptive as I need to be during this explanation. Brace yourself.

You can either picture this as I describe it, or search YouTube for videos of cow inseminations. Believe it or not, there are a lot of videos of this procedure. I'm glad to see that folks out there have the desire to learn. But, I don't need to post videos of me inseminating a cow. There're already many excellent (graphic, but excellent) videos available that are professionally filmed and edited by AI companies to show people how it's done.

I've beat around the bush enough. Here are the nuts and bolts of impregnating a cow.

It starts by gently securing the cow. The cows are placed in a device called a lock-up stanchion, or "lock-ups." The stanchion itself is the opening the cow's head goes through. The opening closes slightly and locks, thereby preventing the cow from backing out. Imagine it looking like a cat that has gotten its head stuck through a fence. It's not tight, but the process of backing through the fence rails to escape becomes problematic.

42

The cow is placed in this restraint for our safety. An agitated 1200-pound cow can do some damage, so we make sure that there are no accidents. She isn't hobbled or tied up; she can move a little, and some lock-ups have food and water within reach of the cow. The person doing the procedure can walk right up to a cow in heat and breed it with absolutely no problems.

Next, the straw full of bull semen is thawed and prepared. The crimped end of the straw is clipped off. The straw is now referred to as the "insemination rod," and it is housed in a container called a "breeding sheath" to facilitate smooth entry into the cow. The assembled contraption is a narrow tube within a tube, roughly two feet (.6 meters) long, and about the width of a drinking straw.

One of the breeder's (me, in this case) arms gets covered up to the elbow (for smaller cows) or up to the shoulder (for bigger cows) by a long rubber or plastic glove. It feels a little bit like Saran Wrap cling film. Think of it like a giant arm condom. The glove needs to be thin enough to "feel" through, so it can't be made of thick material. That covered hand becomes the guide hand.

While holding the breeding sheath in the un-gloved hand, the guide hand and arm is pushed through the cow's anus and into the rectum. A lubricant can be used to make entry easier for both cow and human, especially if the human has big arms like me.

While inside the anus, the guide hand feels around for the cow's cervix through both the rectal wall and the cervical wall. Once the cervix is found, it's gripped in the fist and held steady. This helps to "thread the needle" with the breeding sheath (putting it through the opening of the cervix). In other words, the guide hand needs to be in the rectum because it needs to hold the cervix still.

Think about it like this: it's easier to push a peg through a wall instead of through a mattress. The wall is firm and steady; the mattress would give way and bend or move around instead of allowing the peg to find its way through. If you didn't hold the cervix firm and steady, it would be moving around and nearly impossible to push the breeding tube into the uterus.

Working without a guide hand would mean poking blindly into the depths of a cow's vagina. This would dramatically increase the probability of injuring the animal by easily puncturing the vaginal wall or damaging the cervix.

When the breeding tube is inserted into the vulva, it has to enter the vagina at an upward, 45-degree angle. If the breeding sheath isn't inserted at an angle, the risk of entering the urethra by mistake is high. This would essentially catheterize the cow. The breeding sheath could end up in the bladder if enough of it is pushed in.

Once the angle right, the vagina can be entered. The person performing the procedure cannot see inside of the cow, so they must visualize their hands coming together and the breeding tube pushing past the cervix. Once in the uterus, the still-external plunger is pushed to release the semen.The sperm in the semen begins the journey to find the egg.

All of this is done by feel and experience, which is why the training course is so critical.The course teaches how to do this in a safe, fast, and accurate manner. When I took the course, I trained on the actual reproductive organs of a cow. I suppose the training center could have gotten one made of molded polyurethane, but they retrieved a set of actual innards from a local slaughter facility. From my perspective, there is no substitution for practicing on the real thing. By the time I was certified, I knew exactly how the entire procedure was supposed to feel.

I was 18 years old when I finished the course and completed the procedure for real the first time. Sure, I watched dad do it a hundred times when I was a kid, but he had it under control and certainly didn't need my help.

I had never tried it on our farm prior to age 18 because, honestly, I didn't think I was going to work on our farm long term. My brother was the farmer, not me. He should have been the one artificially inseminating the cows. Or so I thought.

Nowadays, I'm pretty good at it.

My brother-in-law does this kind of thing for a living, so he can inseminate a cow in fifteen seconds or so. I do it pretty often, but not nearly as much as brother-in-law, Dave. As a result, I can do it in about thirty seconds. This procedure doesn't have to be a long and drawn out event. I get in and out as quickly as possible, all while monitoring the cow for signs of discomfort or trouble.

Surprisingly, this is not an uncomfortable procedure for the cow. For many women, having a burly guy shove his arm up your ass while threading a tube through your cervical opening and into your uterus would probably lead to a good bit of discomfort. Being a guy, I wouldn't know that for sure, though, so don't quote me on it.

Honestly, the cows hardly seem to notice. I'm not even kidding.

It's really no big deal for the cow. They are led to the breeding area, their head is positioned through the lock-up stanchion, and they proceed to eat from the feeding trough in front of them. While I do the procedure, the cow munches away as if nothing is going on. When I am done, they are released from the stanchion, finish their snack, and wander off to rejoin the herd. We don't keep them sequestered once they're pregnant. They go about their everyday lives.

We, the farmers, don't decide when we want to breed the cows. It would be nice to line them up and get them all done on the third

Wednesday of every month. Instead, nature decides when a cow is to be bred. They enter estrus, and we jump into action. On average, I probably breed a cow or two per day, sometimes more. With 500 head wandering around, and most at breeding age, you can do the math.

The gestation period of a cow is about six days short of the gestation period of a human. So the mamma cow carries the baby for nine months, and then prepares to birth the calf.

***

Like any birthing process in nature, calving is a painful and rather ugly process. It's not all sunshine and rainbows, that's for sure. I never understood the people who say human childbirth is a beautiful or glorious process. To me, it's gory, gooey, and I hate seeing my wife suffer through something like that.

Horror movie special effects aside, most human deliveries happen smoothly. You've got a healthy pink baby when it's over. For the most part, it all goes well with the cows, too. Their species has been doing this for 10,000 years (University College London, 2012).

Similar to human mammas, sometimes cow mammas need a little help. That help can involve chains and a wench, so the animal rights activists love to play it up. They'll compare the instruments to medieval torture devices. They want you to believe that we are ripping the baby cow out of the mother without regard for the comfort or safety of either one. According to them, farmers are evil sadists at heart, I'm sure. It's no different from everything else animal rights activists claim about us.

In reality, the instruments and protocols we use are implemented to make the birth easier, safer, and healthier for the cows. Once again, think of the cost—but not the way activists are so eager to do. It is a heck of a lot cheaper to prevent and treat problems, and then nurse the cow back to health, than it is to execute the cow, purchase a replacement, and raise it for two years, at which point she is able to begin the birthing cycle.

Healthy cows are productive cows.

***

Throughout the pregnancy, we monitor the cows for signs of normal gestation. We are prepared to handle problems should they arise, but short of those signs, we assume all is going well. Like human mammas, the pregnant cow will live her day-to-day life pretty similarly to how she lives her non-pregnant life.

With the exception of posting belly selfies on Instagram, of course.

We keep detailed records on each cow, so we know when she is getting ready to deliver the calf. Recently, it's gotten easier for us to do this. I'm actually really excited about our new facilities on the farm, so I'll take a second to brag. We now have seven calving areas, making it possible to separate calving cows into smaller groups, with each having

45

her own "birthing room." With this upgrade, I am better able to monitor each birth more specifically.

Before AI allowed us to pinpoint the exact moment of pregnancy, farmers watched for outward signs that the cow was preparing to go into labor. For example, her udder will start "bagging up." That means the udder (like the breasts on human women) will begin to fill with colostrum. Her vulva will swell, and she will start pacing, presumably to encourage the calf's positioning as it readies itself to exit her body. She may be trying to walk off a little of the discomfort, too.

As she gets closer to delivery, she will separate herself from the rest of the herd. Her instinct is to find a protected spot in which to give birth. She and the calf are both vulnerable during the birthing process, so she will be compelled to find a place that minimizes the risk of exposure.

It's nature taking its course.

Once we see her mimic these patterns of behavior, we lead her into the calving area. Here, we can monitor her progress. All is good about 99% of the time. She knows what to do and will do what she has to. More accurately, her body knows what to do. For a human woman's first delivery, she'll tell you about the pain and being little freaked out. But, she knew that baby was making its way into the world, whether she liked it or not. Once the birthing process is initiated, her body takes over and does what it has been genetically programmed to do.

As a result, we honestly don't have to do much while we monitor her calving. Either me, my dad, or a member of my staff will do a quick visual inspection every so often. But the cows are pretty much left alone to have their calves in peace. The cow goes into labor (to use the human term) and the calf comes out with no issues.

The vast majority of deliveries are completely fine; they happen without a hitch. Jersey cows are especially good with delivery. Holsteins have just a few more difficulties than Jerseys. With a Guernsey, it was almost certain something would go off the rails. I don't know why—maybe their size?—but it seemed like there were constant issues with Guernsey deliveries.

To be honest, it seemed like there were constantly issues with Guernseys, period. They are a difficult breed to manage. I swear, they would go out of their way to hurt themselves or find a creative way to die. It got to the point that I would tell people to learn about farming by working with Guernseys. If you can keep Guernseys alive, you are going to make a great dairy farmer.

Of course, problems do come up. Sometimes, the cow will show overt signs of a major medical emergency, such as hemorrhaging, bellowing, or passing out.We might also notice that the cow has been in labor for several hoursand nothing is happening.

Some farmers will wait for twelve hours before putting their hands on the cow and assessing the situation. Generally, I don't like to wait that long. I like to check her after a few hours. I have done this for long enough—and I know my cows well enough—that I have developed a sixth sense for when things don't seem "normal" anymore.

A quick system check involves getting down on the floor next to the cow and either doing a visual inspection of her birth canal, or inserting a hand into her vagina. A good sign is when I can see or feel two feet and a nose. That tells me the calf is positioned properly and is making its way into the birth canal.

Two feet and a nose: All is good and I can leave her alone.

I grow concerned when I can only see one foot and a nose, or any other combination of body parts that is not two feet and a nose. The intervention might be as simple as reaching in, grabbing the other foot, pulling it forward, and positioning it next to the foot that was already in place.

It may sound confusing if you unable to picture what I'm doing. Here's the deal. If it helps, you can compare it to human babies. Picture a pregnant woman lying on her back. The fetus should be facing the floor, with their head toward their mamma's feet and their chin tucked to their chest. This is called the "occipito-anterior" position, and makes the baby's body and the delivery as streamlined as possible.

If the human baby is not in the proper position, the doctor will go through a series of steps to reposition the baby. If all else fails, the mamma will go to surgery, and have a cesarean or surgical childbirth rather than a vaginal childbirth.

The same exact rationale exists for cows. Because of anatomical differences between human babies and cow babies, I have a couple of modifications when I look for the position of the calf. For example, the calf should have both front feet out in front of it. This birthing process is designed to get the calf out of the cow in the best and easiest way possible. The calf's shoulders will be the most narrow when its feet are in front of its face.

Similarly, your shoulders will be their most narrow when your arms are held up over your head. Get the picture?

Let's take that one step further. Whether I see one or two feet, I am also searching for the nose. The feet are obviously critical, but the nose tells me the calf is facing the correct direction. Without a nose, I have no way of knowing whether I have the front feet or the hind feet. In human babies, hands and feet are shaped differently. In cow babies, all I've got is a foot—and all four feet look and feel alike.

If the calf is facing the wrong direction (or "breech," just like when a human baby is positioned butt-first instead of head-first), I know I have to get the calf out of the mother immediately. If I don't work fast, the calf could suffocate before we can get it out.

It's rare for me to reach up there and not be able to figure what the hell is going on. In those instances, I call the vet. I'm pretty good at handling most birthing problems, but I also know my limitations. My goal is to keep the herd healthy, remember? Our veterinarian knows a heck of a lot more than I do, so I have no problem turning the reins over to her.

When we hit a critical condition like this, I can tell right away if the calf is already deceased or not. If the calf is dead, we still call the vet, but we know we have some time to get the body out of the mamma. If the calf is still viable, the vet must hurry to arrive and act quickly to save the life of the calf. During those burgeoning moments, the calf is in far more danger than the mother.

Believe it or not, there is a such thing as a bovine c-section. If the calf won't come out on its own, we can surgically cut the calf out of the mother. This is way above my pay grade! A c-section on a human woman is major surgery. A c-section on a cow is even more complex because of their anatomy. A cow has one singular stomach—contrary to popular belief. However, their stomach does have four distinct compartments. The layout of their stomach in relation to her uterus makes it a tricky surgery. It leaves the cow vulnerable to complications and infections. Therefore, a c-section is best left in the hands of an expert.

A common calving issue is when the calf has gotten held up in the birth canal. If the feet are first and nose is second, all is good there— but the mamma cow may be having difficulty pushing the calf all the way out. While not a worst case scenario, this situation does require human intervention, or else the calf and the mother risk serious injury and possibly death.

If that happens, we use birthing chains or calf-pulling chains to assist in delivery. I'm usually the one who gets called for this duty. To be clear, birthing chains are exactly what you think they are. They are a set of stainless steel chains that get affixed to the calf's front feet.

Pulling a calf is very similar to pulling a car out of a ditch. With a car, we hook the chain to the front axle (assuming the car isn't breech), then use a wench to slowly extract it from the ditch.

A birthing chain looks like the shiny, stainless steel little brother of the huge chains carried by a tow truck. They're made of a lighter gauge steel, and are much shorter—about 30 inches (~75cm) long. If you've ever locked up your bicycle using a bike chain, this one is almost the same size and length. On one end of the birthing chain is a handle that looks like a small, thick-gauged coat hanger. It helps the farmer to have something to comfortably grip while pulling.

I do my best to get the chain onto the calf's wrist or ankle. Yes, I understand that cows don't have wrists and ankles—just embrace the metaphor. Sometimes when I'm feeling around in the birth canal, I may not have the correct angle or correct access to get the chain wrapped in an ideal way. When this happens, I just get a little of the chain to wrap the closest part of the leg and start pulling gently. One way or another, that calf has to come out of the mamma.

We certainly don't yank with reckless abandon. If I can't quite get the chain positioned like I need to, I pull until the calf is far enough out that I can fully see the legs. At this point, I reposition the chains to their proper location on the leg.

It sounds medieval, I know. When I explain this procedure to people, I make sure to emphasize that this is the correct, industry-proven way to put the chains on the calf's front legs. Obviously, we don't want to mess up those front legs. The calf is much larger than a human baby, but it's still somewhat fragile.

Another tool used with the birthing chains is a winch. Believe me, this thing really does look like a medieval torture device. It works much like the winch on a tow truck. When a car is getting pulled out of a ditch, the tow truck uses a winch. It slowly reels in the chain, thereby easing the car back up to the road. If the winch isn't kept taught and steady, the car would roll back down the hill every time the tension was released from the chain.

The winch used for calving is a little different, but uses the same basic mechanics. It rests against the back of the cow, affixes to the grip-end of the birthing chain, and works to keep steady pressure while the calf is being birthed. The whole idea is to keep the process moving forward. We don't want to play peek-a-boo with the calf while it struggles to exit the mamma.

This also happens with human childbirth. Most human mothers have experienced the joy of pushing as hard as she can, only to have the baby recede a little bit when she pauses to catch her breath. The doctor tells her to keep pushing until the baby is out, but if the baby is having a hard time clearing the birth canal, the baby may rock back and forth. It will come out slightly, and then recede slightly, push out slightly, recede slightly. In these cases, the doctor uses forceps (which look like salad tongs to me) or a vacuum suction cup (called a ventouse) to help pull the baby out.

The activists love to take video of the calving procedure and make it look inhumane. Honestly, it's exactly the opposite of inhumane. The reality is that we are working to save two lives.

As I stated in the beginning of this chapter: childbirth is an ugly process in nature. Anyone who has children knows of the sweating, screaming, grunting, and crying involved in a human vaginal delivery.

Imagine how a video of a woman giving birth would be twisted around to make it seem like the doctor is torturing her. Although, I'm sure any woman who's given birth would say it feels that way sometimes!

That's what happens to us in the dairy industry all the damn time. We work hard to make life as easy as possible for our herd. Despite our best efforts, we still get nothing but grief from animal rights activists who distort the truth and play on the heartstrings of people who have no context and no understanding of what is actually happening.

Any time you see a video like that, remember that women go through a lot of mental drama and physical trauma from the time she hits 10cm dilation to the time the baby slides into the doctor's hands.

Was it pretty awful for two to three hours?

It sure sounded like it was.

Was it all necessary?

As far as my wonderful family goes, absolutely—that's how birthing was designed by our great architect.

And finally: Was it all worth it?

Heck, yeah! I have four awesome kids. I am thrilled that their mom (and the doctors) did what they had to do to bring these amazing little creatures into my world.

***

One final thought with regard to calving is in regard to colostrum. Colostrum is the first form of milk produced by mammas following the birthing process. It contains high concentrations of bioactive compounds (mainly antibodies) to give the newborn a fighting chance to bolster its immune system against all the microorganisms trying to infect and kill it. Babies of all species are vulnerable, so their immune system has to be fortified as early in life as possible.

When the calf is taken to the calf pen, she (remember, we try to have all girl cows) is monitored to make sure she gets post-natal medical attention and to make sure she is eating correctly. We ensure all calves receive high quality colostrum to start with.

Because the calf is separated from the mother, we harvest colostrum from the mother and feed it to the calf. If the mother does not produce high quality colostrum, we have artificial colostrum on hand to supplement or replace the mamma's.

Yes, we test all colostrum before feeding it to the newborn calf. It has to be above a specific quality marker in order for us to go ahead and give it to the calf. If it doesn't pass muster, we use an emergency colostrum. We have a stash of good, high quality colostrum if we need it.

Obviously, the best option is to use the mother's colostrum for the baby. In my humble opinion, it seems like the colostrum has evolved to ward off bacteria, viruses, and allergens specific to the environment/

region in which the cows reside. It makes sense to my brain. Common sense has gotten me this far in life. Why change now?

The "artificial" colostrum isn't artificial. In other words, it isn't made in a laboratory somewhere in Connecticut. Rather, it is collected from cows and stored for emergency use. We actually have a pasteurizer specifically for our colostrum, thereby extending its shelf life. Then it can be frozen and stored until we need it.

We harvest the colostrum from new mothers in the same way that human mothers use breast pumps. Then we place it in special one-time-use bags specifically designed to store colostrum, and then throw the whole works into the pasteurizer. Pasteurization is a process that uses heat to deactivate or kill any harmful bacteria and enzymes that lead to spoilage in milk. Milk isn't the only product that gets pasteurized; fruit juice (for example) also goes through this process. The purpose of pasteurization is to extend the shelf-life of the product.

The only difference between the pasteurization process for regular milk and the process for colostrum is that we use a lower heat setting for the colostrum. That way, we can eliminate the pathogens we don't want, but retain the organisms we do want.

People often hear, and sometimes confuse, the terms pasteurization and homogenization. So it might be useful to end this chapter with a quick explanation of each.

The milk you purchase in a grocery store is pasteurized so it can remain fresh for a few weeks as it makes its way from the farm to the store to your dinner table. It also prevents people from getting Salmonella, Listeria, Staph, and E. coli just from drinking the milk (Smith, 1981).

Homogenization, on the other hand, is what keeps you from having to shake your milk jug before you pour a glassful. Similar to pasteurization, milk is not the only product that gets homogenized (I refer you back to the humble fruit juice). If your milk didn't get homogenized, the cream would separate from the rest of the milk. This happens because not all of the fats in your milk are equal in terms of density. Therefore, the less dense fats will separate and rise, like the way oil and water separate. The old adage, "the cream rises to the top" comes from this exact phenomenon.

During homogenization, the milk is forced through extremely fine filters that break up those fat molecules. When every fat molecule is reduced to equal densities, they happily co-exist without wanting to separate. The cream is now mixed in and suspended all throughout the milk and stays that way.

If you have ever been on a dairy farm and taken a drink of farm milk, I will bet they had to shake the milk bottle before pouring. That mixes the cream (which had probably separated) back into the rest of the milk. Without a little shake, you would pour a glass full of very thin milk with little flavor, or a glass full of thick, sweet cream.

On our farm, my parents still drink straight from the tank. They like the milk in its pure form, and more power to them. I'll tell you this for sure: siphoning off the creamy part of the milk makes coffee taste great.

Kaycee wasn't raised on a farm and therefore didn't acquire that taste. She's grown accustomed to pasteurized and homogenized milk. So, that's what we drink. Plus, my kids will sometimes have friends over who were raised on pasteurized and homogenized milk. No sense rocking their world with a new milk. As a result, it is all pasteurized and homogenized in our household.

Chapter 4
Profit is a Four-Letter Word

I have one final unresolved issue regarding the *Dairy is Scary* video. In fact, this issue goes to the heart of the matter. It is the common target that unifies all animal rights activists by providing a foundation for whatever crazy distortions they spread. It is their reason to be—their bottom-line rationale to rally people against my industry.

Money.

A complaint I constantly hear from the trolls online is that I'm only in it for the money. I'm not sure when "having a job in order to make money" became a negative, but for some people it obviously is. I'm WAY too busy to sit around and judge how other people live their lives—as long as their choices don't affect my life. So I don't have a clear understanding of how the trolls manage to support their own families. Apparently, they don't work and don't do anything to make a profit.

I say with all sincerity that I work in order to earn a living. Yes, that means the farm needs to turn a profit every year. Profit allows me to do things for the herd, for the farm, and for my family.

For the cows, profit allows me to feed them, pay the veterinarian to take care of them, pay the nutritionist to keep their diet specific and healthy, and either repair the old facilities or else build new facilities to make their lives as stress-free as possible.

For the farm, profit allows me to pay my employees. The farm supports six employees who have families of their own. To the surprise of social media trolls, my employees are working to earn a living (a profit?) so they can take care of their spouses and children. Weird, right?

With proceeds from my farming profits, I am also funding an enormous upgrade in facilities that will create efficiency in production. Now I can expand my herd and send more milk to everyone's dinner table. If all continues as planned, I can also raise the pay of my employees. Now they earn even more profit and provide even more for their respective families.

Work smarter, not harder, right?

Last of all, profit comes back to me and my family. With the profit I earn from the farm, I can do nice things like buy food and build a house and make sure my kids wear clothes when they go to school. Kaycee drives a car and we have furniture in the living room. You know, we have to purchase things—and these things don't fall out of the sky for free.

Everything in your life costs somebody something. The chair you're sitting on, the gas in your vehicle, and the phone in your pocket all have a price tag attached. Heck, even the air you breathe indoors costs somebody something. If you are reading these words in a building, the air is probably getting heated or cooled (depending on the climate), and that has a price tag attached to it.

Who pays for YOU?

There's no such thing as a free lunch. I prefer to take care of myself and my family, and that requires an income. I don't understand how some people can believe that a farmer—who would like to make money—is evil. On a broader level, a desire to earn a living is somehow construed as an evil idea. It makes no sense, and (once again) leads me to wonder how the activists and trolls pay for the things they consume or own.

If you believe that turning all farming operations over to the government is a good idea, take a look at the history of collective farming. I know that Wikipedia isn't supposed to be a primary source, but it is a great place to start by getting a brief understanding of the subject and using its references for a deep dive into research. A quick perusal at the "collective farming" page will give an overview of government-run agriculture. The Soviet Union, The Ukraine, Romania, Hungary, Czechoslovakia, and many other (mostly communist) countries have not ended with positive results. In fact, some were devastating to the country as a whole. Millions of people died in the resulting famines.

Short-sighted, emotionally-driven people don't seem to be interested in learning from history. Instead of making attempts to avoid the mistakes made by others, they are bent on making the same mistakes themselves.

I don't get it.

At the end of the day, I do not believe that my desire to make a profit makes me a sadistic person. Nor does it make me evil. It seems possible to have a moral compass while you support your family.

But I'm old school that way, I suppose.

And for the sake of transparency, let me run down some of the economics of operating a farm. While I'm sure the trolls think it's all glitz and glamour, I can assure you that I do not lead a rock star lifestyle.

***

Because I run a dairy farm, my main product, milk, is the result of keeping animals alive, relaxed, and healthy. The overhead I deal with is somewhat predictable; my herd consists of living creatures that can get sick, injured, die, or have any number of environmental factors affect their milk production (like the extreme heat I mentioned earlier). I have a good handle on fixed costs and overhead. I have no real control over federal milk prices. But there are some muscles dairy farmers can flex to remain solvent and profitable.

If I were to run a tobacco farm, for example, I would be dealing with crops and not animals. Yet, I would be no more able to fully predict my yield. There is always variability when raising crops because their yield is largely dependent upon the weather. Dry springs versus wet springs; blazing hot summers versus mild summers. Temperature and moisture can be friend or foe. Plus, a hard freeze or two at the wrong time of the growth cycle can be catastrophic for a crop farmer. Also, they have to control parasites, pests, and disease. They have to fertilize, and either enhance the soil with nitrogen or rotate their fields to allow fallow regeneration.

My point is this: it doesn't matter if you're a dairy farmer, a cash crop farmer, or a gentleman farmer with a small harvest. A farmer's costs and profits are never completely within their control. Cash flow must be even to account for some of the ups and downs. Hence, we are all prepared to handle negative situations that will invariably pop up at the least opportune moments.

Some days, I would love to have a regular job where I go to work at eight in the morning and then "leave it at the office" when I drive home at five in the afternoon. I would have health insurance, paid holidays, paid vacation/personal/sick days, a 401k, and the ability to take a "me day" whenever I felt "triggered" or"overwhelmed" by my coworkers or my workload.

Then again, maybe not. I am a farmer, and have enjoyed the freedom of being my own boss, spending time at work with my kids, and working in the great outdoors. In my humble opinion, there is no place as beautiful or as exhilarating as the Tillamook Valley—so why waste all this awesome scenery and fresh air by sitting behind a desk?

It does have its downsides. I am solely responsible for myself and the good folks I employ. That requires a strong business sense so I can make good decisions when deciding how to maximize the financial potential of the farm—without compromising my morals.

Here are some of the fiscal realities I face:

Feeding the cows takes somewhere north of 50 percent of the money I earn selling their milk. That overhead is a fixed cost because a cow's gotta eat. I purchase their food by the ton, so I am granted a volume discount by the supplier. My nutritionist and I make feed decisions. I go into greater detail about nutrition and veterinary care in Chapter Twelve.

Suffice it to say for now, each cow consumes about 80 pounds (~36kg) of food every day. Multiply that number by 500 cows (which will have grown to 1,000 by the time this book is published), and you can see why so much of the farm's income is literally gobbled up by the herd's feed. Even with a volume discount, I still pay for 20-40 tons of food per day.

Labor cost takes somewhere between 15 and 20 percent of my gross receivables. Owning a farm has some tax advantages for sure, but not when it comes to payroll. I pay the employer's end of payroll taxes—and that includes the taxes on the salary that I earn. I don't have the luxury of not seeing taxes taken directly out of my check. Through my accountant, I have to see (and stroke a check) for all the tax money going to our fine government. I wish everyone had to write a check to pay their income tax each quarter, like freelance and self-employed workers do. There would be a lot more people questioning where this money is going. As it stands, their income taxes disappear from their checks before they even realize the money was there in the first place. The IRS found out a while back that a lot less outrage happens when taxes are surreptitiously withheld.

Other fixed costs that I can count on to create monthly overhead: fuel, electricity, sewer, water, and repair & maintenance on existing facilities.

I also pay a local farmer to take care of our feed crops. As of today, we grow 160 acres of feed corn on the farm. That sounds like a lot of corn, particularly if you are comparing our field to the ¼ or ½-acre lot your home may sit on (if you live in a single-family house). From a farming standpoint, 160 is not that big of a number. The value I place on the corn that gets harvested from our 160 acres would not justify the purchase of expensive equipment needed to produce that corn.

I don't have the money to purchase the new-fangled combine harvesters. Even a used one is expensive! It would cost me more in terms of time and money to handle the crops myself than to just pay a guy to harvest it for me with his own combine. Believe me, you would not want to grow a large field of corn without one of these machines.

Harvesting corn requires that you cut the plants, find the ears of corn, shuck them, and then separate the kernels from the husks. The combine harvester does all of those tasks at once. That's why they call it a "combine" harvester. It combines several tasks into one machine.

The bigger and better combines can cost upwards of $750,000 USD—but they are really cool and make life way easier for the farmer. Sure, you could plant and harvest each individual stalk of corn by hand. People did it for centuries. But now we have incredible machines that make our lives easier as well as increase the yield.

The guy who takes care of the family-run farms in Tillamook (ours included) owns two such harvesters. He works the land of almost every farm around the county because he focuses his resources on doing one thing better—and more cost-effectively—than any of us could. He covers around 3,000 acres of corn total. I pay him to do everything that needs to be done for the care and maintenance of my feed corn, from planting the seeds to throwing it in our bunker. It just makes sense with regard to my bottom line.

Farming any kind of crop requires far more than just planting and harvesting. The farmer has to fertilize the soil between harvests, irrigate the crops while they're growing, monitor their progress, and clear away pests.

The farmer who takes care of my corn consults with me when decisions have to be made. We meet or chat over the phone so I can provide input or make a final ruling. That way, I am involved in decisions he makes, but I am not involved with the day-to-day. I write him a check and trust he will get the job done. His fees are a tax write-off for me. At least a little of the cash outlay comes back to me at the end of the year.

We also grow a little bit of grass silage on the farm. Silage is a generic term that refers to anything you might see in bales around a farm field. Silage makes up the bulk of what gets fed to livestock; primarily cows, horses, and sheep.

Cows and sheep are specifically fed silage because of their ruminant stomachs. Ruminants are hooved herbivore mammals like deer, cows, sheep, goats, and even giraffes and camels with a specific kind of digestive system. These animals digest their food twice. I don't mean to gross out any of the readers, but when a cow eats, they regurgitate fermented food from their stomach and then chew it a second time. That's called rumination.

The word "ruminate" comes from the Latin word ruminare, which means "to chew over again." If you are ruminating on a thought, it means that you are thinking about it (chewing on it), moving on to something more immediate (swallowing it for now), bringing it back up in your mind (regurgitating it), mulling it over some more (chewing on it again), and then moving on (swallowing it again).

Same process, right?

I'll go over their digestive systems more thoroughly in Chapter Twelve, but wanted to give some context to silage.

Anyway, farmers can feed grass silage, hay silage, oat silage, or alfalfa. Many grass-like plants come under this umbrella term. These crops are simple to grow and pretty easy to harvest. If you drive to work, you might see fields that look like they are just growing wild. They will be covered in what looks like weeds that grow to be waist- or chest-high. This grassy crop could be any one of a number of plants that will grow, turn brown, and look like a hot mess. The farmer mows it all down, and then runs a baler over the cut crop. The baler packages it into rectangular or round bales.

Once neatly packaged, the bales of silage can be individually picked up, tossed into the back of a truck, and then stored in a barn until needed or sold. Silage is mixed in with summer feed, but is particularly important during winter months when the herd cannot graze on grasses in the pasture.

We grow corn and harvest grass silage on the farm. I purchase alfalfa silage from a friend in eastern Oregon. My goal is to someday own the land and control my own alfalfa, but that's not possible right now. The more self-sufficient I can become, the better I will feel. I might even lose money by growing my own alfalfa, but it would give me peace of mind to know I don't rely on anybody else, particularly during years when alfalfa is a little harder to find.

It's all about vertical integration and self-sufficiency. And it all costs money. There's no such thing as a free regurgitated lunch.

***

I will get an occasional DM flame or have somebody loop me in to a post about how the government is propping up farmers. It's as if some taxpayers are outraged that their dollars are being used to keep our industry—an industry that would otherwise fail on its own—afloat.

As with many of the topics covered in this book, this is one that wears me out. I cannot stop crazy people from lying, but I can shine a light in the dark room of ignorance.

Some people will tell you agriculture is federally subsidized. And if a farm can't make it without these subsidies, it should "collapse." Let's put that statement into perspective.

The total percentage of the 2015 federal budget that goes into "Food & Agriculture" was four percent (National Priorities Project, n.d.). According to the 2014 Farm Act, the "Food & Agriculture" budget was broken down this way: 80% goes to "Nutrition" (for example, food assistance for people), eight percent helps pay for "Crop insurance" (protecting farmers from crop failure), six percent goes into "Conservation" (leaving farmland fallow or turning it back to natural habitat), five percent goes to "Commodities," and one percent goes to "Other" (Economic Research Service, 2014). This money was budgeted for the fiscal years 2014 to 2018 (National Priorities Project, n.d.).

In reality, the vast majority of those "ag subsidies" are actually budgeted government money that goes back into the government to re-write bills and implement pilot programs to re-write the bill. Somehow, this stuff got shoved into the farm bill. Of the $135.7 billion going toward agriculture in 2015 (National Priorities Project, n.d.), $108.5 billion went to government offices and their employees, and 27 billion went to subsidies, insurance, and conservation.Which means after removing the "nutrition" money, agriculture is less than 1% of the federal budget.

58

What is left of that budget that goes to "Insurance" does help with the premiums—meaning farmers only see money during a disastrous loss of crops. Then, the insurance companies pay the farmer, not the government. Trust me when I say farmers would rather have a crop to sell than have it fail and get paid out by an insurance company.

So we get some federal assistance, I suppose—but it is not the windfall that activists suggest it is. Have farmers been given money to help offset the costs from trade wars going on? Yes. Would farmers gladly not receive them and just be able to sell their products? Yes—but we also understand that the government is an aggregator that negotiates and brokers those international deals. They try to stabilize the global market and balance forces that may be trying to drive down prices.

You know what? I wish I made more of a profit than I do. When I back out all the money going to overhead, it is disappointing to see how much is left over, particularly given the amount of work I do around here on the farm!

***

Water is a basic necessity and is constantly in demand for farmers. I'm glad we run a modest-sized dairy farm. Our needs pale when compared to some of the larger grow operations. Some of the big farms you'll see are running 50-100 irrigation circles (also known as central pivot systems, or water wheels) at a time.

The irrigation circles are giant devices that provide water to fields of whichever crop the farm is producing. They are long overhead sprinklers on wheels that extend from a center (pivot) point. As water is forced through the sprinkler heads, the entire arm rolls 360 degrees around the pivot point. The most common ones are ¼ mile (~500 meters) long, and make lush green circles against a backdrop of brown (or less green) fields. They're pretty cool to see from an airplane flying overhead.

Because we don't grow cash crops, like cotton, soybeans, alfalfa, corn, or tobacco on the farm, we don't invest in elaborate watering systems. In fact, the climate in Tillamook provides plenty of rainfall for our needs. We get close to 100 inches (~254cm) of rain each year, spread pretty evenly throughout the calendar. So the feed crops we grow on our farm are mainly watered the old-fashioned way. We do irrigate the pastures for a couple months out of each year, but we are fortunate to live in the best climate on Earth.

We also have water rights to the Wilson River and pull most of our irrigation water from that renewable source. Plus, there is a large ground-water pond on the farm. The pond is likewise a renewable source, given the amount of annual rainfall in our area. We'll occasionally pull water from the pond as well.

Don't forget that cows drink a lot of water, particularly when you compare their needs to the needs of a human. Our cows take in around 40-60 gallons (113-151 liters) of water per day, depending on the weather, of course. We raise Jersey cows, which are smaller than other breeds of dairy cow, so their needs are slightly less than if we raised Holsteins or Guernseys.

Our barn and our parlor where the cows are milked are both on the Tillamook municipal water system. That way, we don't have to worry about water contamination or parasites in what the herd drinks.

We still pay a water bill like you do at your home. However, we don't fret about water as much as crop farms in more arid climates like the Midwest. But we need to maintain the pumping systems we have established from each of those sources, and that requires overhead. There are costs for equipment, parts, labor, and time lost from other endeavors, that gets calculated in to our water budget.

No such thing as a free ruminated lunch. Or a free gulp of water.

***

Keeping food and water in mind, we have another fixed cost. It's sort of a dirty little secret in the dairy industry. Kids are fascinated by it when they visit the farm, but adults turn up their noses up to it.

What do we do with all the poop and pee?

Before you read the next few paragraphs, you may want to put down your sandwich. It's not for the faint of heart.

If you have never seen a cow poop and pee, it may shock you when it happens. The cow lifts its tail and unleashes a blast of urine and manure. When I am walking a group of school children through the barn, I love watching their faces when a cow lets go of its bowels. A roar will go through the crowd, followed by abject stunned silence, followed by laughter and a bevy of jokes among each other.

The cows don't seem to care what or who is going on around them when it's time to let loose. Invariably, at least a couple of the cows will photo-bomb one of my videos with a fetid fountain of waste. Sometimes I wonder if they hold it in and wait for me to pull the phone out of my pocket. I'll be trying to talk about an important issue, while getting drowned out by the sound of wet manure splattering against concrete.

It's positively delightful. And each cow poops two or three times per hour.

Yeah. Barn boots are a must. So are good reflexes.

Hyperbole aside, you can imagine how much waste is produced by a cow. They eat a lot, drink a lot, and don't get a ton of exercise to burn it all off. On average, our Jerseys produce around 100 pounds (45kg) of manure per day. Dairy farms with larger Holsteins or Guernseys will deal with even more per cow.

If you're wondering how a cow can turn 80 pounds of food into 100 pounds of poop, remember that their food goes in dry, gets mixed with 40-60 gallons of water, and then comes out as a soggy mix. It'll put a spring in your step when a cow fires a geyser of that stuff in your direction.

And the urine? They discharge about three gallons (12 liters) of urine per day.

I won't continue to astound and horrify you with the statistics, but it's safe to say we have to constantly deal with cow waste. Not just because of the unpleasant smell; if you allow the waste to marinate in the barns and common areas, it can invite disease, flies, and other nasty elements that affect the health of the herd. So we take the necessary steps to get rid of it.

The floors of the barns and parlors have troughs, flush systems, and drainage furrows (similar to a sewer system) built in. Those move a lot of the waste along, but the walkways have to be cleaned and maintained separately. For those areas, some farmers have a poop Roomba. We don't have one yet, but it will be nice when a few of those bad boys are zooming up and down the alleys 24/7.

Okay. It's not exactly a Roomba. But it's close enough. For the sake of accuracy, the technical name is "auto-scraper." Just like a Roomba, these are robots that patrol the walkways and passages, cleaning as they roll along. They are smooth, relatively quiet, and get the job done. Humans still have to go through and sweep/hose down areas to keep them cleaner, but the bots do most of the heavy lifting.

Once the waste is collected, we store it in tanks. Some bigger farms create a "poop lagoon" to cut down on overhead, like building the tanks or storage facilities. You probably don't want to eat what you catch if you fish in a poop lagoon.

(Sorry. I'll probably erase that last sentence before this book gets published.)

Once it's stored in the tanks, we use the manure for fertilizer. Cow poop is high in nitrogen, thereby making it an ideal (and natural) fertilizer. It also has a number of other nutrients that aren't available in the soil. Even though I stand ankle-deep in it on most days, suburbanites will spend good money on bags of cow manure fertilizer at their local Home Depot.

Some farms—particularly the big ones—will use the waste to generate electricity. I don't...yet. We will probably look into that process once all the new facilities are figured out and we are in a good rhythm with the bigger herd and the new way of doing things.

On a more pragmatic note, our climate does not allow for much evaporation to happen in the barn. Plus, when we pump the liquefied waste into our holding tanks, that same moisture is trapped in the tank with the solid waste (again, no opportunity for evaporation). This high moisture content allows us to eventually spread (or spray) the manure onto the growing fields.

For manure and urine produced in drier climates—and particularly on farms that have a poop lagoon—a good bit of the moisture naturally evaporates from the waste. In fact, some of the huge farms can afford to invest in separators (which separate out the solids) and evaporators (that turn manure into consumer fertilizer). These farms produce enough manure that they can effectively monetize the waste.

My understanding is that the technology exists to separate the nitrogen and phosphorous from the waste. That gets a little over my pay grade, but I think it's pretty cool. We just don't produce enough waste to justify the cost of such equipment.

Manure is such a perfect fertilizer, a war was once fought over it. I'm not even kidding.

In 1865 and 1866, The Chincha Islands War (also called The Pacific War or The Spanish-South American War) broke out between Spain and the combined forces of Peru, Bolivia, Chile, and Ecuador. In a nutshell, Spain sailed in and seized the Chincha Islands, which were rich with bat guano. That pissed off the South American colonies. The farmers needed the guano to efficiently farm and fertilize their land. This war was the bloodiest ever fought on the western side of South America. Nonetheless, it ended in unlikely victory for the South American forces.

If you get a chance, pick up a copy of The War of the Pacific by Gabriele Esposito. You'll never look at poop the same way again.

***

Once in awhile, I'll get a tersely-worded comment or message on Facebook from someone who uses biblical justification to attack me. I'm not sure how to navigate the irony of weaponizing a religion that basically teaches people to love thy neighbor, but I will leave my parochial ideas aside for the moment.

They go on and on, telling me that money is the root of all evil. They add that I am sinful and that I will burn in the eternal fires of Hell if I don't change my hedonistic ways.

I'm not sure how they could afford the phone or the computer they just used to type that message to me. As much time as they spend online, they couldn't possibly hold down a job. If money is evil, then they must not like to have any. Oh, well. Let's forget that paradox so we can analyze their argument.

It seems to me they didn't read their Bible very closely. Granted, I'm no biblical scholar, but I do know how to read. I'd like to point out that, according to the New King James Version, 1 Timothy 6:10 says, "For the love of money is the root of all kinds of evil." Almost every modern translation of the Bible states it similarly. For me, that means that money, in and of itself, is not evil—the love of money is what Timothy said was evil. We should give to Caesar what is Caesar's, but don't covet the cash.

Tracing the history of money is nearly impossible, thanks to the poor record-keeping of so many complex civilizations. We don't even have a record of any society that used only barter (Surowiecki, 2021). We do know this: people figured out what had value and what did not. Our ancestors would trade with each other to get what they'd need to survive.

But, trading can be tricky. One person may be in need of some arrowheads and he has a bag of dates. To start, he needs to find someone who has arrowheads. Then, he has to find someone who has arrowheads and who wants some dates. That's a tall order right there.

To keep trading fair, the use of money as a medium of exchange came into play. Our person can now simply trade the dates for some gold coins. He can then take the gold coins and exchange them for some arrowheads. These gold coins were a form of commodity money. This type of currency has value in and of itself. In colonial America, beaver pelts and dried corn were used as commodity money—those items had an intrinsic value (Investopedia, 2021).

The United States stopped using commodity money since we were taken off the gold standard in 1971. Today, we use a form of currency called fiat money. Fiat money has no intrinsic value. Its only value comes from our faith in the government and our country. It gives our economy some flexibility and it's cheap to produce (Chen, 2021).

I know this is a very simplified history of currency; I'm no economist. But, here is what I do know for sure: to get by in this society, you need money. It's how we trade in a modern world. However, if your entire existence, your only goal in life, is to amass more and more and more currency—hoard it at the expense of your community, family, or health—then the Bible would consider your actions to be sinful.

I don't live that way. Sure, I like nice things (and I know Kaycee does, too), but money is only one part of my overall life plan. I have goals that may require money to achieve (go on a cruise to Alaska, for example), but I also carve out ample time for my friends, my family, and my interests that have nothing to do with dairy farming.

I try to lead a balanced and healthy lifestyle.

To put my work in perspective, if my primary objective in life was to be rich and powerful, there is no way I would have gone into dairy farming. I would have taken a very different path. My chiseled good looks and fierce animal magnetism (plus my extraordinary humility) would have paved the way to being a leading man in Hollywood action films.

But I digress.

Hopefully, you now understand the basic mechanics of overhead within a dairy farm. Even better, I hope it didn't make your head explode.

***

Just as much as money goes out, it also has to come back in. Let me share a few morsels about capital inflow. First, this section represents only the tip of the iceberg. The macroeconomics of market fluctuations and the forces that push change in federal milk prices are extremely complex. Second, keep in mind I can only tell you what I know from my own perspective and experiences.

The Tillamook dairy community is a great group to be a part of. Its origin story is even better. My family settled here from Switzerland because my great-grandfather, Alfred Josi, thought the climate in Tillamook was ideal for raising dairy cows. Numerous small dairy farms existed at the time. They banded together in 1854 in order to purchase and/or build a schooner, a kind of covered wagon, to transport their milk and butter over the mountains that surrounded the valley. Portland was a prime market for their wares. Thus, they decided to make more money and improve their lot in life by selling to the people of Portland.

In 1909, these local dairy farms officially formed a co-op, the Tillamook County Creamery Association (TCCA). They hired an ad agency and started to market their product even further down to the coast of California (Todd, n.d.).

This simple action increased their customer base. A bigger customer base meant more money. More money allowed for expansion and improvements of the farms, the herd, and their families' futures. The co-op grew, and it eventually included all the dairy farms and farmers in the region. To this day, we are still a regional co-op; all of our member farms (about 80, as of the writing of this book) live and work in the Tillamook Valley.

If you have ever driven through a rural town, you have probably seen co-op stores. In them, you'll find many of the basic necessities for farmers. They'll sell feed, fencing, tools, dry goods, specialty items for their region, and probably some lumber. It's like a tiny Wal-Mart for the farming community.

Most people think that "co-op" is synonymous to the stores they run. However, the most important function of a co-op is to serve in the best interest of the farmers. Think of them the same way you think of a labor union. And yes, labor unions get a bad name because there have been

64

widely-publicized examples of corrupt union leaders getting arrested and charged with racketeering (among other felonies), famous strikes that have interrupted commerce, and early on, some historic events that led to violence and bloodshed between unions and management.

Like the co-op, unions exist to protect workers. They are responsible for negotiating and maintaining better working conditions, better pay, better benefits, and clearly defined work weeks.

For example, the United Auto Workers was formed in 1935 in Detroit to protect auto workers (United Auto Workers, 2015). The automotive industry was exploding in the U.S., and corporate executives weren't looking out for their employees. Factories and the assembly line configuration had been in America since 1901 (Corday, 2014), but conditions hadn't kept pace with human needs.Factories were dirty, hours were long, and workers had no legal cap on the number of hours they worked. It was a rough life, man.

The UAW allowed the workers to be represented as an entire mass rather than as individuals. Strength in numbers, right? With that collective strength, they were able to negotiate better pay, a sensible work week, and benefits, such as health insurance. There was also safety in numbers. The union pushed back if the company did something that negatively impacted the workers. If the company balked, the workers would strike as a unit. The UAW balanced the power of employer and employee.

I'm not advocating for or against labor unions. I just believe that everything exists because it's useful to some capacity.

Dairy farmers, like all farmers across the United States in the early 1900s, worked as individual fiefdoms while our country grew. They had no collective power because, for the most part, there wasn't a national market. The farmer grew crops or raised livestock, and then peddled their wares locally.

As the markets expanded and transportation improved, farmers were able to sell their products in bigger cities. There, they were at the mercy of merchants that wanted to buy low and sell high. If rural Kansas farmers wanted to sell their beef in Wichita, they had to abide by the rules, both economic and legal, set forth by the merchants in Wichita. The farmer had no real power. If they didn't "play ball," they were snubbed in Wichita.

It was more or less the same situation in Tillamook. Our valley was dotted by dairy farmers, many of whom were trying to get their milk, cheese, butter, cream, and everything else into other markets so they could expand. In order to do this, they competed with each other to get into stores, sell for the lowest price, and figure out how to more effectively distribute their own dairy products (for example, build their own schooners).

However, if all the dairy farmers combined their forces, they could achieve wonderful things. Creating a cooperative (or, the co-op) would mean consolidating their small farms into one powerful unit that could create a common infrastructure of a distribution network, negotiate milk prices on behalf of the entire group, and provide resources for farmers to help each other out. This help would include a general store and a meeting place where farmers could discuss trends, issues, and share wisdom or life hacks.

I know this was a long-winded history lesson. But everyone needs to understand the background in order to understand how incredibly important the co-op is to local dairy farms in general, and to my farm in particular.

The Tillamook County Creamery Association has leverage when it comes to selling our products. Consumers like—and need—what we produce, so we are able to set our own price for milk. However, we don't get drunk with power; we do our best to keep our prices in line with the federal milk price.

The federal milk price is what the government pays for milk. Buyers nationally tend to conform to the federal guidelines. This means the government has tremendous power when it comes to determining the price at which we sell our milk, even if it isn't sold to government agencies. It's similar to how the Federal Reserve tinkers with interest rates. Banks will adjust their local interest rates based upon the guidelines set by the Fed. Similarly, milk markets adjust their pricing based upon the milk fed.

We price our milk along the lines of the federal pricing structure. However—and here is the important part—if federal prices dip, our co-op stands its ground by maintaining the price at a higher level. In a down market, they do their best to make sure we still make the same amount of money when we sell our milk. This protects our members by allowing us to better predict what we will earn.

It also protects us from market fluctuations. If the fed decides the government price for milk falls by one dollar per hundred weight (more on this in a second), we can stick together and refuse to drop our prices at that same rate. We have some muscle, and flex it occasionally when we need to protect the livelihood of our members.

Let me tip my cap one last time to the TCCA. Our co-op in Tillamook has been fantastic. Believe me, I talk to farmers all over the country, and not every co-op is created equal. Some grow too large to notice the needs of local farmers. Some have disorganized or unfocused leadership. Others just don't do much at all. Ours has been on point for as long as I can remember. The TCCA does right by its members. They're focused on producing a high quality product that brings in revenue to the farm owners.

This is beginning to feel like a college classroom. Don't worry; there's no final exam.

I mentioned that we get paid by the hundred weight. That sounds like a complex unit of measurement, but it is exactly what it sounds like: one of this unit equals one hundred pounds (~45kg) of milk. The rest of the world went metric back in the 1980s. Our industry, like our country, has held onto the old British Imperial, or United States Customary, units of measurement.

I know it's strange to think of selling milk in terms of weight (pounds) rather than in terms of volume (gallons). You purchase liquids by volume, we sell by weight. This is probably to avoid shady behavior by sellers, since weight is a more accurate measurement than volume. Weight is a measure of how heavy an object is. Volume is a measure of how much space an object takes up.

I'm sure everyone has opened a bag of potato chips, only to find the bag is only ¼ full. If you purchased chips by the bag (volume), you'd feel ripped off and be angry. If you purchase chips by net weight (3 oz.), then it doesn't matter what size container they come in. Three ounces is three ounces—even in a big, mostly empty bag.

It's the same with milk. Weight is weight, no matter what container it comes in.

I am writing this book during the summer of 2021. As of right now, the federal average for milk sits somewhere between $18-20.00 USD per hundred weight, depending upon cost of production and which region of the country you live in. That price is adjusted monthly based upon market trends and the demand for our products. From my point of view, it is what it is: this is a frustrating way to price a product that I'm pretty sure will never change.

In order to translate this into your price at the supermarket, let's do some quick math.

Each gallon (3.78 liters) of milk weights approximately 8.6 pounds (3.9kg). Divide 100 by 8.6, and you get 11.6, if you round down. Therefore, 11.6 gallons (43.9 liters) of our milk sells for roughly $19.00 USD. Break that down per gallon, and you get $1.64 USD.

Currently, farmers are paid around $1.64 USD for every gallon of milk they sell.

As of August 2021, the retail price of whole milk per gallon is $3.71 USD (Agricultural Marketing Services, 2021). The difference between what I get paid and what you end up paying goes to the government's tax coffers, the packaging facility that puts the milk into cartons and jugs, the distributor who warehouses the milk and delivers it to stores around the country, the individual truck drivers who drive the transport, and last of all, the owner of the Piggly Wiggly who sells you the milk.

Everyone down the line has to get paid.

The co-op oversees all of these transactions. Our milk is sold through the co-op, so they connect us with buyers, collect the money, keep all the records for us, and then write each of the farmers a monthly check based upon the sales. They are also responsible for marketing our products, and have a long-term vision of growing our brand and expanding our business. The co-op makes other profits for us as well, like running the store. Each farmer member receives a quarterly check based upon those profits.

In this capacity, the co-op acts like the agent of a professional athlete. The agent hypes the athlete, negotiates deals with the team, takes care of business and personal needs of the athlete, and collects and distributes the monies. The agent works at the pleasure of his or her client, but is always making decisions and acting in the client's best interest.

We farmers like to gossip and complain sometimes, but our co-op has no horrific Jimmy Hoffa-type of history. Each farmer is a voting member, and things are run above board. We have a director and a board of directors, and they are elected to their positions by the farmers.

The co-op does its thing, and we all benefit.

It certainly helps that we have such an incredibly good product. Our milk, cheese, and ice cream are second to none. Because of that, our milk is in high demand. If we had a product that nobody wanted, our prices would have to drop, or else we'd never sell anything. As long as people want what we have to offer, we are able to keep our pricing structure favorable to the members of the TCCA.

In all honesty, I have no earthly idea how the federal government sets their price for milk. I'm fairly convinced there is a monkey in a back room somewhere in Washington DC who throws a dart at a spinning wheel. Whichever price the monkey's dart hits, then that shall be the price of milk around the United States.

I joke, but am probably not far from the truth. I have never met anyone—including government employees who work in that department—who quite knows how it all works.

When the federal milk pricing program began, vast majority of the milk was sold for fluid consumption (i.e., to drink). Now, we have Class 1 milk to drink at the dinner table, Class 2 milk for blends, Class 3 milk for cheese, Class 4 milk, and so on.

It's monkeys in a room throwing darts at a chart. I'm sure of it.

***

I said this earlier: I wish I earned a bigger profit.
There. I said it again.

Does that make me a bad person? Depends on who you ask. Ironically, I'll bet the same people who throw stones also wish they lived in a nicer glass house.

Don't get me wrong; I am not against activism as a whole. There are definitely some worthy causes and good people who do their best to make the world a better place. But, follow the money. Some of these organizations extract millions of dollars by triggering people's emotions. The administrators of the organizations, in turn, will siphon off a huge chunk of that donated cash, with little (if any) money going to the actual cause.

Even individual YouTube personalities who make their living attacking other people and their industries can make hundreds of thousands of dollars from ads, affiliate programs, and donors. Rage sells, and they are the shopkeepers.

I admire their ability to monetize their bullshit, but I seriously doubt they truly believe all the crap they are spouting. The more outrageous and extreme, the better it sells. So they conjure up ways to get more and more outlandish so they can draw in more viewers to pump more cash into their Patreon or Paypal accounts.

It's another great irony that the people who make their living trying to convince you that they "care so much" are the same people who don't give a second thought to the folks whose lives are being negatively impacted or destroyed by their lies and distorted messaging. It's dog-eat-dog, baby. And if they can capitalize on ruining your family's future, then they absolutely will. They cast you as the villain so they can act as the hero. And if the "villain's" future is slain, then that's probably what the "villain" deserved anyway.

I'm getting irritated. It pisses me off that good people are manipulated to donate money to these scam artists. As I write this, I am AGAIN reminded of why I do all these videos and put up with all the crap from online trolls. Dairy farmers (and farmers in general) are not the problem. We're not the bad guy who strokes a white Persian cat with prosthetic metal hands while our henchmen construct a nuclear Death Ray in our lair. No, doctor. We feed the world. It is our livelihood, and it is our calling. It's also not bad to work harder or have a desire to better our financial situation.

Not all farmers can afford more efficient ways of farming. Some of the smaller farms can't afford newer equipment and technology. Plenty of family farms still do things the "old-fashioned" way. For the most part, we squeeze every nickel out of being efficient and cost-effective. New can be expensive! I'm sure there're going to be more technological advances in the future, but my DeLorean is a few ticks short of 1.21 gigawatts. Most of the time, we can only work with what we have available at the moment.

Our new facilities will allow me to milk more cows for the same amount of labor cost, which is made up of money and time. You often hear the phrase, "Time is money." It's true. I pay my staff based upon units of time. The less they are able to do during that time, the less productivity I see for the money I pay them.

Talking round numbers, the new facilities will save me roughly one mortgage payment per month. I'd tell you what I pay in mortgage for this farm, but it would depress both of us.

More lactation stations in the new barn allow me to separate the cows more completely, thus saving me more time. This allows me to feed new mammas a post-calving diet that is specific to their individual needs. The high-producing cows get a high-energy feed. This keeps them healthier. Tail-end/dry cows have their own rations designed for maintenance and calf health. In the old facilities, I was not able to individualize feed in the lactation area. Rather, all cows might have gotten the high-energy—and highly expensive—food.

With an additional 500 cows, which doubles my herd, I am also buying twice the amount of feed. Bulk purchasing means I can pay a lower price per cow for their food. Walmart can sell a box of cereal for less than the local market. Walmart purchases millions of boxes at a time, whereas your local grocer just buys dozens. Walmart pays significantly less and passes some of that savings along to the consumer.

A cow can only produce so much milk. To be honest, you can get your cows to produce more, but those extra few pounds of milk will cost you more in feed. This trade-off might cause you to actually lose money. We try for the sweet spot, whereby we get the most (and best quality) milk in the most cost-effective way while still maintaining the health and well-being of the herd. Those data points all come together at the place we try to hit every day.

Some cows can and will overeat if we let them. They aren't exactly like horses, which are notorious for over-eating if they get into the grain. We allow our cows to free-feed, which means they can wander over to the trough and eat whenever they feel so inclined. But like a human, cows can find themselves eating too much over time if we don't monitor their calorie intake.

Somewhere along the way, cows became synonymous with being overweight ("You're a fat cow!"). Dairy farmers don't want fat cows. Fat cows cause you to throw money down the drain with regard to feed cost. More importantly, a fat cow will compromise its health. Fat cows have fatty liver issues, just like with humans. Fat cows will also have calving issues. I could go on, but you get the picture.Skinny cows are not healthy cows, either. They can suffer from the same amount of issues.

Cows do have an ideal weight, and we work hard to keep our cows within their target weight zone. Remember: Healthy cows are productive cows!

Chapter 5
A Day in the Life of a Dairy Farmer

I know the activists want you to believe that I sit around all day, twirling my mustache and dreaming up new ways to abuse my cows. To dispel that myth, I figured I would walk you through an average work day. It starts early and keeps me pretty busy, so I think you will find there is very little time left over to devote to abusing cows.

I wish I could say my day starts at the crack of dawn. Nothing could be further from the truth. My day actually starts so far before the crack of dawn, I'm almost ready for lunch by the time the sun yawns and stretches and rolls out of bed.

2:30 a.m.

My first alarm goes off. I know you think that was a typo; nobody in their right mind would willingly get up—seven days a week—at 2:30 in the morning. If it makes you feel any better, some days I sleep until 2:45.

True story. My first alarm goes off at 2:30. Most days, that's all it takes. I lumber around in the dark and get dressed without incident. On other mornings however, I will Frisbee my phone against the wall and go back to sleep. On those days, I wish I was an activist so I could sleep in and take a little "me time" whenever I felt "overwhelmed" or emotionally triggered.

In my world however, work has to be done.

If I do fall back to sleep, the secondary alarm goes off at 2:45. At that point, I have no choice. If I am not up and moving around, I am fully aware that my dad will call to tell me I'm late getting to the barn.

So I do what has to be done.

2:40 a.m.

I am dressed and downstairs, pouring a cup of coffee. I take it with cream, in case any of you are wondering if I am consistently a dutiful dairy farmer. And let's face it, why wouldn't you put cream in your coffee?

With coffee in hand, I am out the door. While my truck is warming up (I drive an old diesel and we live in a cold state), I check private messages on Instagram and Facebook. Nothing starts the day better than a bevy of nice messages telling me I am a horrible person who abuses animals.

Coffee doesn't energize me nearly as well as anger or frustration. Or rage. Which would be a great brand name for my future coffee empire. I can hear the slogan now: Start your mornings with RAGE!

Okay, not really. But I do check messages (and respond to most of them) because, as I mentioned earlier, 95% of the people I deal with online are good people. Some of them are pretty darn funny and interesting to interact with, so I devote a little time to them every day. If there are too many to get through by three in the morning, I'll table the rest and slowly poke through them all by 6:00 in the morning.

3:00 a.m.

I am in full work mode. I go to the barn first, giving cheery 3:00 a.m. greetings to my workers. Not even kidding. I am the chipper little worker bee every morning. Some of my workers arrive on the farm at 2:30 a.m., and I want them to know they are appreciated.

If the boss skulks through the workplace with a grey cloud over his head, that attitude will demotivate the workers. It also destroys morale if the boss seems to hate his or her job; misery is contagious. If the boss isn't willing to do the heavy lifting, that can be off-putting, too. I won't be the type of boss that expects everyone around them to work while they lean on a shovel. You've all probably had that boss; the one who makes work environment as miserable as can be. I try to be the boss that adds energy to my workers, not takes away from.

Two of my workers are there at 2:30, setting up the parlor and getting ready to milk cows. Cows get milked twice per day; once in the early morning, and once later in the afternoon.

On small family-run dairy farms back in the day, the family members—including the children—got up early to do chores, such as milk and feed the cows. Then, the kids would go to school...and when they'd come home, they'd repeat step one.

That schedule is no different these days. The major difference is that we have technology to expedite the milking and feeding processes. With a farm as large as mine, there would be no way to complete all the chores with just the members of the Josi family. We are fortunate to have the ability to pay workers to help carry some of that burden.

I arrive at a fully prepped barn and meet my dad. During warm-weather months, he and I bring groups of cows in from pasture. During cold months, the cows are already indoors and ready to be led through the milking process.

When we get to the parlor, my workers intercept the cows and the milking begins.

At this point, I start cleaning out stalls in the barn. My dad is perfectly willing to do this task, but I don't like him doing it. At his age, I would rather let him do something less labor-intensive instead of bending over and cleaning stalls by hand. He'll jump on the scraper tractor and clean the alleys or walkways between the stalls.

The alleys get splattered with poop and pee because of their juxtaposition to the cows' hindquarters. When the cow is in her stall, she typically faces inward. Her rear-end is positioned in an outward-facing orientation. When she lets loose, the excrement is deposited into the alley.

It's most likely to hit directly behind me when I am trying to shoot a video.

We are still waiting to get our poop Roombas. It's the little things that make me happy.

I get the stalls nice and clean and fluffed up for the cows. New straw replaces the old, and it genuinely gets fluffed up for them. Like a concierge at a five-star hotel, I offer turn-down services for my ladies. And they appreciate it.

The milking is underway and going smoothly. If there are issues creating a slow-down or disruption in the process, Dad or I step in to remedy the problem. It's usually Dad at this point, because I have to jump in the feed truck and begin mixing the first load of feed for the cows.

This part of the morning tends to go like clockwork, so I roll through it pretty quickly. Obviously, anomalies may alter the plan, but both workers and cows know the drill. We work together because all of us want the cows to get milked and fed.

4:00 a.m.

Food preparation begins. I'll give an overview of what a cow eats in Chapter Six. It's more complicated than you might think. And because there are several components, or ingredients, in cow feed, all of the parts have to be mixed together.

Cows are exactly like people when it comes to eating. If all the components of this dry "fruit salad" aren't thoroughly mixed, they will pick out the yummy stuff first. They nose through it and eat the grain, then leave the rest behind. It's like a human picking all the M&Ms out of a bag of trail mix. I'll get to the bottom of the bag and notice there are no M&Ms left. Then I'm angry, and I probably won't finish the bag.

Because the cows won't get a balanced diet if they are left to their own devices, we mix the food so that it's nearly impossible for them to eat selectively. Each mouthful will contain a good combination of the nutrients they need.

It takes about an hour to mix the feed. Afterward, I go back at the barn to distribute the feed. We don't feed the cows by group; we get all the feed in front of all the cows at once. They have to get milked in groups because the parlor is only able to handle so many at one time, but the feed doesn't work that way. We have a big vat of food with an auger that pushes the feed into the trough as the cows gobble up those first bites. Then, they are free to eat at their leisure.

A number of people have let me know they think I am a horrible person because of the feeding videos I have posted. The auger shoves out the feed at a pretty fast clip, thereby causing it to cascade down. Some of the cows get excited at feeding time, so they'll bum rush the feed bunks. Then they place themselves directly into the line of fire as the auger showers them with a sluice of food.

For anyone interested in what really goes on, here it is: the cows are free to back up at any time. I don't torture them by tying them down and burying their heads in a mountain of feed. They choose to be there because they want to be first in line to grab some chow. For a cow, it probably feels like diving into a chocolate fountain.

As the feed is getting pushed out (and sometimes on) to the cows, I sit in the truck and watch. Most people don't understand how much information a farmer can gather by paying attention to the cows during feeding time. You pick up a lot of intel by seeing which girls are coming up to the feed bunk and which are not.

If a bunch of cows are lying down after they've left feed in the truck, I'm probably over-feeding them. This alerts me to pull back on the amount I'm feeding them.

I can also spot individual problems. If most of the cows are wandering over to eat, but one remains behind in a stall, something is up with her. I'll jump out of the truck to check on her. She might need attention immediately.

If you think I'm just joyriding in a feed truck, let me tell you it's more complicated than that. Sure, it can be fun to drive a feed truck, but the health and well-being of my herd is my top priority. I take care of the cows, and they take care of me.

While Dad and the workers are rotating new groups of cows through the milking and eating process, I hop off the feed truck and tend to the fresh cows in our hospital area.

The term "fresh cows" refers to cows that have special needs. The vast majority of those cows are calving or have just calved. They are called fresh cows because they are "fresh" into their milk.

Fresh cows can be in our hospital for many other reasons and maladies. If they require medication or monitoring, this is the part of my day dedicated to them. Obviously they might have needs that may extend beyond this window, but each of the girls will get whatever they need.

During an average week, about seven to ten cows are in that part of the barn. Most of their common issues can be addressed at five in the morning.

6:00 a.m.

When all the morning's loose ends are tied up, we get a break in the action. The cows have been milked, fed, and any special needs cared for. They are then free to wander around the farm and do whatever it is they do. Some graze, some rest, others congregate around the water cooler (trough) and gossip about how wonderful Derrick is.

I know this because I eavesdrop on their conversations. I also speak fluent "cow."

Back to reality.

Most days, I use this break to sit down with my parents and chat over coffee at their kitchen table. We talk about the farm, the town, relatives, politics, news stories—whatever tidbit seems to be most topical in the Josi family. Mom might pass around a plate of muffins, but I try to save my appetite for breakfast with Kaycee and the kids, which comes later. I enjoy these moments. My folks won't be around forever, so I take advantage of the time I get to spend with them.

Speaking of caring for familial needs, at 6:30 every morning, I text my wife, Good morning, Beautiful. I may not hit 6:30 on the nose, but I never miss a morning. I don't need an alarm set for that; I remember the old-fashioned way every day.

Kaycee might not be awake when the message lands on her phone, but I find she gets upset when I forget to do it. It's something simple that means a lot to her. I certainly mean every word of it; thus, it gets done.

Marital advice from the dairy farmer. You read it here first.

***

I mentioned that I have coffee with my parents on most days. On other days, an issue may come up that requires our time and attention. A blown septic tank, a leaky water hose, a bovine medical emergency; big working farms have a lot of structural components, any of which can fail at the most inopportune times. Dad and I are the last line of defense, so we handle whatever pops up.

Incidentally, these days I try to use the six o'clock hour to exercise. I vowed that the summer of 2021 would be the time I get in better shape and lose some weight. It's hard to build a consistent regimen around my crazy schedule, but I am pretty stubborn once I make a decision. I don't go to a gym. I go for a walk. Our property is vast, our valley is beautiful, and our weather is ideal. So, I walk.

For a few days each week as I walk, I'm on the phone with Steve, the guy who is helping me write this book. Because I am doing so many things, I don't like to waste time. If I can multi-task, I am absolutely going to multi-task. I'll shoot a video while driving the tractor. I'll reply to private messages while I am waiting for feed to mix. I'll talk to my ghostwriter while I am walking.

Work smarter not harder, right?

7:00 a.m.

I start feeding the heifers. They get special food that has to get mixed and delivered separately from the rest of the herd. Think of it as puppy chow versus regular dog food.

8:00 a.m.

By this point, it's time for me to eat something. I've done a lot of work, but it's not yet time to power down and relax. It's time to join the morning ritual in the other Josi household.

At eight o'clock, I'm walking through my door, way too awake for my wife. She's been dealing with two young children since the moment they bounced out of bed. Kids can go from zero to 100 in the lift of an eyelid. Most likely, the kids woke up a good thirty minutes before Kaycee would prefer to have gotten up.

The girls wake up anywhere between seven and seven-thirty. They have amassed a full head of steam by the time dad walks in, and I eagerly enter the fray. I love spending time with my kids. I am their playmate, their disciplinarian, their teacher, their mentor. I am their dad.

I take that role very seriously. I wrote about how my parents aren't going to be around forever, so I try to experience as many memories as possible with them. Likewise, my kids won't be home forever. They grow up, learn to fly, and leave the nest, just as they are supposed to. That day will be difficult for Kaycee and me. Until then, I am going to experience the full range of fatherhood—the joys and the sorrows—because I know it is so important to the little faces that look up at me and smile every morning.

I'm not much of an emotional guy. I'm a dairy farmer. I deal with issues of life and death every day. I have to. We, as a farming community, have to. But when it comes to fatherhood, I am extremely passionate.

My dad was always around for me. He still is, in fact. My phone rings throughout the day and it's Dad telling me he needs this or that, or maybe a cow has wandered off, or we have an issue that requires immediate attention. I get annoyed sometimes, but it's my dad's voice on the other end of the phone. Just as it has always been. When I grow annoyed, I lose sight of how important he has been to me throughout my life. When my mind returns to center, I appreciate all he has done.

Like my father before me, I am not "trying" to be a good dad. I am a good dad.

***

I am in the house, messing with the girls while Kaycee sips her first or second cup of coffee. God bless her. She needs a solid jolt of caffeine to help her deal with a husband who's already one full tankard of coffee into his day, and has been up hustling for five-and-a-half hours.

When the family's unbridled joy of seeing me walk through the door has died down (hey, I need to tell myself this—don't take it away from me), I start cooking breakfast.

And I LOVE cooking breakfast!

By the time most people have been up for over five hours, they are ready for lunch. I don't eat a whole lot before eight in the morning, despite getting up at 2:30. I might grab a granola bar as I am running out the door at 2:45, but I am fueled by coffee until I sit down at the table with my wife and children.

Not only do I love breakfast, but I love cooking breakfast. I will whip up a small compliment of kale and egg-white omelets, complimented by organic fruit medleys and a chilled yogurt parfait.

HAHAHAHAHAHAHA! Sorry; I couldn't finish typing that with a straight face.

So, nope to that. I cook biscuits and gravy, hash browns, bacon, and scrambled eggs, with the doggone biscuit gravy slathered over the top of everything on the plate. I am hustling for fifteen hours every day, and need food that will stick to my ribs.

Unfortunately, it also sticks to my waistline. I look at pictures of me at 19 years old, and wonder who stole that body and replaced it with this one.

We all sit down at the kitchen table and eat breakfast together. This touches on the same concept as before. Kaycee and I will miss these days when they are over. So, we take advantage of it while it's here. It's not only for our own pleasure; these moments instill values and a moral compass in our kids. Those values will extend into their own parenthood ideology and passed down, hopefully, to their kids.

If those values aren't passed down to their own children, Grandpa (that's me!) will make sure they are.

9:00 a.m.

When breakfast is finished and the mess cleaned up, I watch the girls for a half hour while Kaycee goes out and works our horses. Her task is very much like walking a dog every day. Horses, like any animals

79

(humans included) need exercise as a part of their daily regimen. Kaycee makes sure our horses stay healthy, just like I make sure our cows stay healthy. We are responsible for the animals we raise.

You've heard of dog people and cat people trying to coexist in a crazy world; we have a similar issue in our marriage. I'm a cow person and Kaycee is a horse person. Her grandfather and grandmother were among the first members of the Western Horsemen of Oregon, a gaming association.

One of the first things she ever said to me, on that fateful evening, back at The Schooner (the bar where we first met) was, "Look...I have horses. If that's going to be an issue with you, don't waste my time."

She must have worked her way through a few losers before she met me.

We currently own two horses, which is cool. As the kids grow older, we'll almost certainly acquire a couple more. Don't get me wrong; I love the horses, but I'm still not completely sold on becoming a horse guy.

To be honest, I feel bad for the horse when I ride. I'm a big guy, and figure the horse is thinking something like, Urgh...what did I do to deserve THIS?

But, as husbands everywhere can probably guess—I earn big brownie points when I suggest that she and I take the horses and ride them down to the beach.

So Kaycee gets some horse time and I get some kid time. And that makes us both happy.

9:30 a.m.

When Kaycee finishes with the horses, she returns to the house and rescues me from the marauding horde of girls who are trying to overthrow me.

Just kidding. Sort of.

But, when Kaycee comes in, I try to take a 90-minute nap. Sleep is a commodity I value, because it is so scarce in my life. Having young, energetic children can tax the most robust of spirits because they wear away at the sleep time we need as adults.

Moms certainly have it worse; they have the milk that babies demand at 1:00 a.m. feeding times. And they hear those demands because of their Mom Ears. Kaycee is nothing if not a protective mother. Even if I get out of bed to attend to the kids in the middle of the night, Kaycee is awake (at least a little bit) and concerned about the cause (and outcome) of their distress.

I do my best to try to steal an hour and a half nap after breakfast. My belly is full, the coffee is starting to wear off, and I am ready to crash.

Obviously, sleep takes a backseat to everything else I have to do: a farm emergency, a kid issue, or some other obligation might preempt my nap. But more often than not, I go to bed and catch a few z's.

I don't need the nap. But when I do take it, I am far more fresh at the end of the day.

11:00 a.m.

I set an alarm to rattle me out of my nap. No sense being tardy to the second shift of my work day. At 11:00 a.m., I return to civilization.

Awake, I help with the kids again. Most days, their late morning/early afternoon has a rhythm. As a result, so does mine. When the kids enter the jet stream that pulls their day along, I attend to farm business matters. For the next two to three hours, I attend any meetings I have and do any paperwork related to our financial operation.

The animal rights activists might be surprised to hear this, but we are monitored very closely to make sure we are following protocols and managing our farm ethically, legally, and humanely. We have inspectors from our own organizations and inspectors from various government agencies who schedule times to swing by and check up on us. The inspectors drive out and need a chaperone to walk them around the grounds and show them whatever it is they need to see. We sell food products, so the FDA must make sure our processes, fixtures, and equipment are up to par. We raise livestock, so we have to demonstrate that we are doing so in a humane manner.

We are currently building new facilities, so the building inspector is regularly on the farm to check our progress. I keep up with veterinary records, financial records that get audited, and employee safety manuals we must update and have on hand. I order any food, supplies, and equipment we need, then balance the farm checkbook.

As much as the activists want you to believe we're vile, cold-hearted leviathans that terrorize a sea of helpless cows, we never operate outside of the watchful eyes of agencies set up to protect the animals and your milk.

Once all the administrative work is done, I monitor the numbers for my online presence. While posting videos on Facebook is not my full-time job, I am constantly tinkering with different ways to maximize my presence. That requires some analysis of their algorithms. I also keep stats on what I post, how many people it reaches, and what the interactions look like.

2:00 p.m.

By two o'clock, I'm back in the feed truck, mixing food. Cows get fed twice per day—roughly twelve hours apart. The food remains available for the entire twelve hours so the cows can eat whenever they feel hungry.

Like any animals, they fall into a routine and tend to gather when the chow truck arrives.

They also drink water freely throughout the day. Our water troughs are auto-fill, so there is a constant level of water for them at all times.

It takes about 45 minutes to mix a full load, which will feed the entire herd for about 12 hours. More accurately, a load will feed them for 12 hours during pasture months. During winter months, when the herd does not supplement its feed with grazing, I feed them three loads of feed each day. It's still two feeding sessions, but there's more food per meal.

Thankfully, mixing doesn't require constant attention. I have some time to make a video, return DMs on social media, or spend a little time with one of the kids.

3:00 p.m.

The afternoon schedule is a carbon copy of the early morning schedule. The only minor difference is that I don't have to feed the heifers again in the afternoon. Otherwise, I mix food, I deliver food, Dad and I move cows through the milking parlor, I clean stalls, I tend to fresh cows, and I take care of any odds or ends that pop up when running a large mechanical and livestock operation.

I would estimate that 75% of my days move pretty smoothly. Because I work seven days per week, every week of the year, at least one or two days each week I get thrown a curve ball. Our employees are very good at following directions, but some things that need fixing require the boss to diagnose and resolve. Dad takes some of that burden from me, and he will cover if I am out of town or unavailable. For the most part, I am the bottom line on farm. I have the final say and take responsibility for anything that I don't feel can be handled by an employee.

5:30 p.m.

I return to the house and have supper with the family. By and large, I am interacting with family at 5:30. We eat, then have the evening to relax and unwind. People occasionally ask if I have hobbies or interests outside of dairy farming. To that I answer, "Uh, yeah...sure."

I always hesitate because my answer sounds like a total cop out. But, it's the God's honest truth. My family is my hobby! In addition to evening time, I do my best to attend their activities; baseball games, school activities, the County Fair. I often fail because the farm is an extremely demanding workplace, but I am there as much as humanly possible. Same with my folks—Mom and Dad are good grandparents. My children are not for want of family.

There isn't anything I would rather do that to spend time with my wife and children. I really don't watch television; I have more productive things I could be doing with my life. I'm not all that into sports, and I am not interested in any activity that requires "tinkering," like building projects, working on cars or motorcycles, hunting, fishing, and so on.

If pressed to come up with something I enjoy as a "hobby," I would say that I like to read.

I know—totally nerdy, right?

Well, don't judge. I particularly like to read historical fantasy and science fiction. I like the work of quite a few authors, like David Weber & Terry Brooks, Robert Jordan, and David Eddings. They are my escape from reality when I need to unplug my mental switchboard and power down for the night.

Unfortunately, I can get too wrapped up in a book and find myself reading until late into the wee hours of the evening. The next day, I feel like a train hit me; a giant fictional fantasy train filled with lost sleep and images of dragons and broadswords.

I must admit that do sit down and watch the major sporting events (The Super Bowl, for example). I'll also put some eyeballs on sports highlights from time to time. I was a pretty good football player back in the day—and even had an opportunity to play some football in college. But these days, I think people spend too much time immersing themselves into statistics, players, drama, and fantasy football. Frankly, I would rather watch a sporting event live in a stadium full of people than waste time watching it in my living room.

"Down time" is scarce in my life. So, I try to make every minute count.

9:00 p.m.

I try to be in bed with the lights out by nine o'clock. With small kids, those plans sometimes go awry. Barring a miracle of epic proportions, we will not be having more children. As my daughters grow and become more independent and self-sufficient, my life should ease up some. But for now, Kaycee is pretty good about making sure I get proper rest. She is busy as well, but wants to keep me sane and healthy.

My best case scenario: I get five and a half hours of sleep at night. Combined with the 90-minute nap I try to get in the middle of the day, that rounds it up to seven hours total. Dairy farm work is divided into two shifts which are governed by milkings and feedings.We have to be ready to work early in the morning and then later in the afternoon. In my experience, short sleep combined with a nap is the most effective way to juggle that schedule.

Quite frankly, for my constitution, seven total hours is the perfect amount of rest. I am a well-oiled machine if I get my seven hours each day. If I fall short, it feels like I am running around with half of my nuts and bolts missing.

...

I should probably rephrase that.

If I fall short of the seven hours of sleep, I run around all day feeling like half of my screws are loose.

...

That probably didn't sound any better.

Conclusion

That's my day, every day. It will change on the rare occasion we take a small vacation. Kaycee and I try to get away on a trip together (just her and me) at least once per year. We also try to do something each summer with the kids.

When I am away from the farm, I wish I could say I didn't worry about the farm. For now, Dad takes over and does an understandably masterful job of keeping things running smoothly. He will very occasionally blow up my phone if something happens that gets him excited. For the most part, he lets me have my time away. He makes it easy for me to not care as much.

And if I'm being honest with myself, that part will never change because my dad is never going to die. He may retire someday, but he shall not pass away.

Don't ruin this for me.

If Dad does decide he ever wants to retire, it will be more difficult for me to completely cut loose mentally when we are away.

So, I get on the same treadmill every morning and do my best to be a productive member of society. Unfortunately, a part of that means taking on the trolls.

It's a frustrating, ugly job, but someone's got to do it.

And I'm The Man.

Chapter 6
4-H and FFA Are Not Terrorist Organizations

I can't believe I have to take time to discuss this issue. Yet, sad to say, some activists are trying to sell us on the notion that 4-H and FFA are terrorist organizations.

Slap your forehead alongside mine as we dive in.

A big part of my childhood was participating in both 4-H and FFA. I have nothing but fond memories.

It all started one Christmas....

Some people can remember their fourth birthday party or their kindergarten class or the day they first set foot in a Chuck E. Cheese. I don't have a lot of memories from those earliest days of my life. In fact, the earliest incident I can remember clearly was Christmas morning, 1991.

I was eight years old, excited to see what Santa left for a kid who was obviously good for the entire year. Farm kids reading this book will immediately understand that opening presents is a luxury only indulged after morning chores are finished. My sister, brother, and I knew the routine. It wasn't an imposition; it was just life.

Out to the calf barn I went. I was nothing if not dutiful, as much as an eight year old could be. When I entered the barn, I saw a Holstein calf with a halter, tethered to a spot in the middle of the barn. It confused me; this wasn't a part of the routine.

As it turned out, she was my Christmas present! I fell to my knees and patted her head. She was mine...and that was special. My mind raced with plans of showing her in contests around the state. Entering "judging contests" at county fairs and state expos was a rite of passage for farm kids. Pigs, goats, sheep, animals large and small would get cleaned up, transported to the fairgrounds, and proudly shown by farm kids wearing their Sunday best. We were dairy cow people, so Holsteins, Jerseys, and Guernseys were our animals of choice.

Frankly, Jersey cows are more popular to be shown by children. Jerseys are the smallest breed of dairy cow. Being small makes them ideal for seven-year-old girls to lead into the judging pen.

Holsteins, on the other hand, are the largest breed of dairy cow. While many Jerseys struggle to top the 1,000 pound (~453 kg) mark, Holsteins routinely weigh around 1,500 pounds (~680 kg). Holsteins are the most popular, and most easily recognizable, breed of dairy cow. When you picture a dairy cow, you probably picture a Holstein's distinct white-and-black pattern. Their size can make them a difficult task for small kids to wrangle, thereby making the Jersey a more common choice in judging contests.

Early on, my parents recognized that I was big for my age. I was a husky kid by any standard; tall and "filled out." So instead of having me dwarf a poor Jersey cow—which would not have made the cow look good to the judges—they got me a Holstein. A big cow with a big kid.

We were a good match, although I honestly can't remember how we did in the contests we entered. It was just fun to be a part of the show. I learned about competition, camaraderie, and cows. The three C's of my development as a dairy farmer—and as a man.

***

A more apt title to this chapter might be "Kids in Agriculture." I can't think of a more wholesome concept—nor one that is nobler—than kids learning about agriculture. In my humble opinion, teaching kids about the basics of human sustenance is a good idea. Maybe I'm just a delusional, money-grubbing sadist (as I have been accused of being several hundred times on social media), but the foundation of our existence boils down to how well you can take care of yourself and your family. Food, water, and shelter are basic biological needs. How do you grow vegetables? How do we raise and care for animals? How do you build stuff? What is the value of hard work?

This is a no-brainer, right?

WRONG!*

*according to animal rights activists

An inexplicable group of these activists work overtime to churn out content aimed at convincing their audience otherwise. They claim these organizations are terrorist plots to indoctrinate our children into the warped cult of The Dark Side.

You know what? I'm not even going to joke around with this anymore because this is such a willfully ignorant attitude. These activists genuinely do preach that 4-H and FFA are terrorist organizations. Their words; not mine. Their logic falls apart because it cannot support its own idiocy, but they love to beat that drum.

Here is the problem: I have watched these videos go viral. I don't think anybody in normal society is duped by these nonsensical ramblings because they are so far over-the-top. In the end, they are summarily ignored or laughed at.

Still, messages like these really chafe the agricultural community. In fact, they chafe to the point that agriculturalists all over the world begin to share the videos in an effort to point out how the activists are dead wrong in their ideology.

Unfortunately, we have become the face of our enemy. In a strange twist, our community seems unintentionally responsible for a lot of the reach the activists have achieved. I have seen some of their web sites and social posts. Their message falls totally flat on their own platforms. A typical post of theirs gets two or three likes by their followers, and little else. They have no traction on their own.

But antagonize farmers, and BOOM! We will jack the activists' numbers to the moon. Everyday people ignore and scroll past, but farmers share.

The more inflammatory their video, the more outrage among farmers, and the more the video gets shared. It's brilliant in its deviousness and insidiousness. The activists are nothing if not cagey.

This is my strategy: I take one of their videos, hack it up, splice in my commentary following each of their stupid points, and then repost the video as my own. So now when the ag community starts to share, they share my video instead of the activist's distorted propaganda. Their message still gets through—it's embedded in my video, of course. But not without a proper reality based, accurate counterpoint to each of their dumb, unsubstantiated, and often WRONG points.

In other words, I use their own strategy against them. Thank you, Sun Tzu.

***

The agricultural community is a proud community. We are proud of our roots, our hard work, and our families. Our children can grow up in an environment that extolls the values of roots, hard work, and family. For generations, farm families were large families. There was a lot of work to do, so the children began helping at a young age. The more children a farmer bore, the more help he had around the family farm.

Now, consider how our country grew up. Once the industrial revolution began, our population was divided into two groups: city folks and country folks. I don't use either of those terms as pejoratives. I mean them quite literally. City folks went to work at factories and businesses that supported the families who lived in the city. Country folks continued farming and agricultural endeavors, or ran businesses that supported the agricultural community. They provided all of the food for themselves and most of the food for the city folks.

When you add in the fishing industry, farmers and fishermen together provided all the food for city folks. It wasn't a bad thing; it was just the way it was. Agriculture was a way of life, not a career path.

For kids who grew up in the country, they grew up in farming families and went to school with the children of other farming families.

School schedules and activities tended to bend around farming schedules. Morning chores and afternoon chores were essential at home, so school days morphed their schedules to fit between those lines. Summers were busy and winters were less busy (particularly for crop growers), so they adopted the school calendar. The kids had summers off, and then they hit the books during the dark months.

Likewise, extracurricular school activities catered to the agricultural community. Hence, 4-H and FFA were born.

These two organizations have an interesting and storied history. You can certainly read about it by visiting their respective websites, 4-h. org and ffa.org. For the sake of brevity, I'll give a short overview of both in order to provide some context. All of the information I am sharing can be found on their websites.

The 4-H organization has been around since 1902. The moniker, "4-H," refers to their original motto: "Head, Heart, Hands, and Health." It has since expanded into an updated motto:

I pledge my head to clearer thinking,

my heart to greater loyalty,

my hands to larger service,

and my health to better living,

for my club, my community, my country, and my world.

Their mission is to "…engage youth to reach their fullest potential while advancing the field of youth development." It has grown into a worldwide organization and strives to educate kids, and their families by extension, about the fundamentals of agriculture through both practical and hands-on learning. They also try to connect public schools to rural life, even in urban settings.

Using encouragement and empowerment, 4-H teaches the proper way to interact with animals, grow vegetables, can and preserve food, and compete with other kids in ag-based competitions. The organization helps these same kids develop self-esteem, confidence, responsibility, and compassion, along with very valuable life-skills.

FFA originally stood for "Future Farmers of America." It was founded in 1925 with the mission of supporting and promoting agricultural education through classes in middle schools and high schools. In 1988, they changed the name to "National FFA Organization" to reflect the growing diversity in agriculture.

I don't disagree with the mindset here—the organization wanted to expand the public perception of their reach. It's no longer solely geared toward farmers. Now they are involved in teaching kids about the science, business, and technology of food, fiber, and the natural resource industries. It's now about much more than farming, and that's a good thing. It's about every industry that supports farming, too. Technology is making farmers' lives easier, and the current-day FFA embraces it.

Agriculture and all of the science around it is not only "nice" to have, but it is absolutely critical to our survival. Farming is food. Whether you are a carnivore or a vegan, your food originates from a farm, not a laboratory. Even Soylent Green was organically based!

I really hope that made you laugh, because it was a joke.

These two organizations exist solely to teach kids about food and farming. Whether that education is hands-on or instructional, kids learn to respect the source of their food and find out what it takes to plant, nurture, and procure that food. Along the way, they learn about animals, plants, and the hard work that goes into raising them.

So 4-H and FFA deal with all aspects of all kinds of farming. But let me bring this back to the activists, who attack everyone in the industry. I've talked to enough farmers to know that beef cattle ranchers, hog farmers, chicken farmers, and anyone else who raises livestock for a living get attacked online, too. Crop farmers have their own special kind of online trolls to deal with as well. Dairy farmers aren't alone here; we are merely part of the Axis of Evil, according to the animal rights activists.

Tying these concepts together, a favorite ploy of animal rights activists is to show a series of photographs taken at 4-H or FFA functions. First, they show kids with their animals. Rabbits, pigs, cows, or whatever animals they have. The pictures reflect the high emotion of excitement and pride in those children.

Then, they cut away to pictures of children with sad, crying faces. They proclaim that this is what happens when the children learn their favorite animal is going to end up on their dinner plate.

You know by now that this story line is completely cooked (pardon that awful pun). They concoct their twisted narrative, and then find whatever images they can that fit their narrative. They don't show actual footage of the parents ripping the innocent animal from their child's sweet grip and maniacally laugh as their prize bunny rabbit or favorite doe-eyed calf is massacred, boiled, and served as stew for supper that night.

Would you like to know why they don't show video of that exchange?

Because it doesn't happen like that!

Who knows why those kids look sad and cry in the "after" pictures. Maybe they fell and hurt themselves. Maybe someone stole their ice cream cone. Maybe they didn't win a ribbon and they were disappointed. Maybe the photographer at the photoshoot told the hired kids to pose that way for his client. Who knows?

Life does has moments of pain, shock, and sadness. Let's allow our children to feel the emotions. Let's teach them how to manage the loss and understand the realities of life. Let's remind them that we love them and want them to never go hungry. That way, they aren't a hot mess when they get older and have no concept of how to handle disappointment or rejection in the real world.

But I digress.

The activists pull photos of children experiencing emotions, then shoe-horn those photos into their agenda. A kid is happy? They are showing their animal. That same kid is sad? Because someone told her that her calf is going to be slaughtered.

Obviously.

Then the "activists" swarm social media, boosting Facebook or YouTube posts with comments of how disgraceful it is to capsize the children's hopes and dreams this way. They rant about how cruel 4-H and FFA are because they pull the curtain back and indoctrinate young children to the harsh way that farmers abuse animals. They go on a tirade about how kids are being desensitized to the inner emotional life of the animals, thereby forging the next generation of sociopathic animal abusers in the fires of 4-H and FFA.

Empathy is destroyed. Nurturing is destroyed. The innocence of youth is destroyed. Thanks to these organizations that brainwash farm children into growing up as gleeful murders of helpless animals, they will end up just like their family before them.

What a load of road apples.

I'll give you the reality of these organizations, and the reality of how they positively influence the lives of the kids who participate.

In my humble opinion, these organizations are amazing at teaching youth the skills of critical thinking. Even in urban settings, kids learn how to grow edible plants in their own homes. They also learn how canning and preserving these foods keeps them fresh for later consumption. The ability to store food makes us more independent because we are not burning energy and resources searching for food every day. Even during a scarcity, we can have some on reserve.

These organizations teach the scientific method. They teach kids to evaluate the outcomes of decisions they make, which is a big part of critical thinking.

My daughter is raising a male pig for 4-H. As part of the project, she has to keep track of how much she feeds him and how much daily weight he gains. In order to compete in shows, she has to make sure the pig is no more than the maximum weight allowed, based upon what is healthy for the pigs. Hers was gaining a bit too fast, so she had to adjust his diet to keep him within the healthy limits.

The kids learn good life skills, but they don't realize they're learning because it's fun. Embedded in the mechanics of the curriculum are several learning experiences. The organizations sneak in those valuable lessons!

By raising this pig, my daughter is learning algebra by calculating the pig's weight, growth, and dietary serving sizes. She learns proper nutrition for her pig and the life skills of being consistent with his feeding and maintenance schedule. By competing in shows, she learns to be on time and to be prepared. She is gaining self-confidence whenever she walks out in front of the crowd and learns to carry herself with poise and self-respect. She will learn to be a gracious winner when she wins and a good loser when she loses.

Her school can fill in some of those skills, but that system of education can't do it all. Hands-on life experience and working her way through difficult tasks are the best way she can develop all of those life skills. Her 4-H experience provides the total package. From a dad's point of view, I could not be more proud of her.

Although I'll be ticked at the judges if she loses. But that's just me. That is a joke, just so you know.

***

Give me a moment to shock you. I hope you're sitting down.
The activists are correct.
Bet you thought I'd never say that.
Those knee-jerk emotional pictures activists show of children crying? Yup, those are correct: kids are going to be sad when they learn that animals die.

A part of 4-H and FFA—in fact, a part of owning any animal—is helping kids understand the life/death cycle. When you acquire a dog, you know you are going to outlive the dog. Barring anything unforeseen, you adopt that dog knowing full well that you will someday have to deal with the death of that dog.

Nobody talks about it. Nobody likes to think about it. But that's the way it goes. Do you deny yourself the richness of owning a pet solely so you can avoid the sorrow following its eventual death?

I hope not. I know I don't—I love dogs!

Do you prevent your child from getting a dog or a cat because you want to avoid having a difficult conversation with them? Are you going to just dodge your kid when their pet gets ill or passes away? Do you want to ignore their grief?

Again, I hope not. Even though I'm not a big fan of cats. To each his own.

But, that's my big point. Somewhere along the way, you will have to make time for a little sit-down with your child to talk about life and

91

death—whether it is for a deceased pet, a terminally ill grandparent, or a family friend who perishes in a car accident. Death is a part of life.

With all of our animals on the farm, death is a part of their life cycle, too. Even if we take the statistic I mentioned earlier in this chapter—that cows live to 20 years of age—that means we will have cows dying every week in our herd of 500 or 1,000. Much like they figure out the reality of Santa Claus and the Tooth Fairy, my kids will figure out that cows die.

Their beloved animals from 4-H will die, too. Whether they die naturally or they are euthanized, the child will outlive the animal. Is it best to wait until that day to finally talk with your child about death? Good lord, I hope not! Let's help them prepare for the grief and help them have a cognitive and emotional structure within which to understand and cope with the loss.

Emotional preparation—it's not just for people who grew up in the 1970s.

So, yes; we do talk with our kids about the circle of life. And yes; the kids are still tremendously sad when an animal they love dies. I'm glad they are sad. That means they have empathy and that they can attach emotionally to other creatures, including humans. I like that they can experience the full range of emotional awareness, and can live comfortably with the fact that their life will occasionally have sad occurrences. They can weather the storm because they have those internal resources.

That is our job as parents. To prepare our children for real life. Thankfully, we have 4-H and FFA to help us out.

***

I get lovely comments regarding teaching children the realities of the farm. My Facebook comments includes gems like, "When are you and your wife going to slaughter your children and eat them? Because that is what you are doing to the cows."

Okay, let's get a grip, folks. If this was an audio book, I would play a needle scratching across a record. Or tires squealing to a stop. As they said on the old late-night Ginsu Knife commercials, "But wait—there's more!"

State lawmakers are being influenced by animal rights activists to make livestock farming downright impossible to not only work for a living, but to share that knowledge with our children. In my opinion, this is no accident.

The fuss began with a ballot initiative in Colorado called Initiative 16. It sought to revise a section of the state criminal code, 18-9-201, that defines cruelty to animals (Geiger, 2021). Thankfully, the Colorado Supreme Court found the language in the initiative to be misleading and incomplete. Thus, on June 21, 2021, the court removed it from the

November 2022 ballot on the basis that, "...the initiative's expansion of the definition of sexual act with an animal would criminalize additional conduct regardless of whether that conduct is directed at livestock or other animals..." (Colorado Supreme Court, 2021). Great news for Colorado farmers!

Not so much for us in Oregon. A similar ballot initiative is in the works here called Petition 13. This initiative attempts to make artificial insemination illegal. Activists already make the practice sound as disgusting and emotionally wrenching as possible. Granted, it's no picnic for farmers either, but Petition 13 takes it a step further. It's framed as a sexually perverse act.

The initiative reads,

"Section 6. ORS 167.333 is amended to read: (1) A person commits the crime of sexual assault of an animal if the person: (a) Touches or contacts, or causes an object or another person to touch or contact, the mouth, anus or sex organs of an animal or animal carcass for the purpose of: (A) [a]Arousing or gratifying the sexual desire of [a person] either party; or (B) Breeding domestic, livestock, and equine animals as defined in ORS 167.310..."(Oregon Secretary of State, 2020).

The phrasing doesn't name artificial insemination specifically, but it stands to reason AI is exactly what is referred to.

Petition 13 adds another layer to this supposed "sexual assault:"

---

*"Section 4. ORS 167.325 is amended to read:...
(c) The person knowingly commits the offense in the immediate presence of a minor child and the person has one or more previous convictions for an offense involving domestic violence as defined in ORS 135.230 (Definitions for ORS 135.230 to 135.290). For purposes of this paragraph, a minor child is in the immediate presence of animal neglect if the neglect is seen or directly perceived in any other manner by the minor child (Oregon Secretary of State, 2020)."*

Let's think this through. Add the overlay of how we pass this knowledge down to our kids. So, if we accept that AI is a depraved sexual act, then we are presented with even broader ramifications. If we expose children to artificial insemination and teach them the protocols and procedures, we are thereby exposing children to lewd and sexual acts (Oregon Secretary of State, 2020).

If I am assisting in a particularly difficult calving, I could also be considered a sex offender. Technically, I would be touching the cow in their "private parts," which would, according to the ballot initiative, be legally defined as a sexual act. And then, if one of my children is there helping or observing, I am exposing them to a lewd act (Oregon Secretary of State, 2020).

If you can't tell the difference between artificial insemination (or calving) and bestiality, there has to be something seriously wrong with you. I described the AI process earlier in this book, and I will repeat this because it bears repeating: there is NOTHING sexual about the AI process. It takes 15-30 seconds, and every farmer does it because they have to, not because they get their jollies doing it.

I am not blind to the fact there might be some cases of bad apples out there in our community. Every profession has its fringe element. But once in a while, we'll hear a news story about a physician sexually abusing patients. Do we thereby abolish the entire medical profession because of the abhorrent behavior of a small number of its practitioners?

Hell, no. We punish the offenders and accept that the other 99% of doctors are following the Hippocratic Oath by using ethical standards.

It blows my mind that people who know nothing about farming are making laws that affect the lives of farmers. As a result, I strongly suspect that these ballots have nothing to do with farming itself, and more to do with advancing the agenda of animal rights activists.

We could do away with AI and get back to breeding cows the good ol' fashioned way. Yes, it would be less efficient and less cost-effective for the farmers, but it would also be way more dangerous for the cows. The decisions we make as farmers are based upon the notion that healthy, low-stress cows are productive cows. We try to arrange their lives to be as pain-free and as stress-free as possible.

Let's consider the conversation between a farmer and his son or daughter about cattle reproduction. Would you rather be a farmer explaining the process of artificial insemination, or a farmer explaining what's going on while their kid sees a cow getting violently jumped by a bull in the pasture? Just...let that awkward image soak in.

***

I have written earlier in this book that we send the cows to slaughter when their milk dries up, but before they become too infirm to walk into the slaughterhouse itself. Contrary to the insane prattle of the animal rights activists, I do this out of compassion. Yes, it's possible for a business to be compassionate.

Profit is a small part of it; dairy farming is my business, and I have to treat it as such. We simply cannot afford to continue supporting cows that no longer contribute to the overall well-being of the business.

On a very pragmatic level, if I don't watch the bottom line, the whole bottom falls out of my farm and my livelihood. That may sound harsh, but that's the reality of it.

On a compassionate level however, slaughterhouses provide a lot of food for our nation's people who suffer from food insecurity.

Yet, the animal rights activists refuse to own up to their own hypocrisy. Sanctuaries, the very bastion of self-righteous people who say they are altruistically answering "a calling" to care for abused and neglected animals, need a continuous flow of money to operate. What happens if donations dry up and they can no longer afford to care for the animals?

This is the truthful answer nobody likes to hear: the animals will die of starvation and neglect.

Like Mother Nature, I make sure to keep the herd culled. It is in the best interest of the cows. I ensure that conditions are kept safe and comfortable for them. We give our cows a very good life. Before their health has a chance to go downhill as they age and suffer, we end their life in a quick and humane way.

This is a part of farming that I have made my peace with.

If you'd like to know more about humane slaughterhouse processes, I highly recommend a video series produced by Temple Grandin called *Glass Walls*. She examines slaughterhouse procedures with different types of livestock. Most of the episodes are on YouTube. They are well done, stark in their presentation reality, but balanced in how the information is disseminated. Best of all, Temple Grandin is a champion of animal welfare and has worked hard to balance compassion and pragmatism in the industry.

***

I've mentioned how difficult death is for children. Death sure as heck isn't any easier for adults. As of this writing, I'm 38 years old. I know how the life and death cycle works, and I accept it. But, that doesn't change the fact that the worst—the absolute, gut-wrenching worst—part of dairy farming is when I have to euthanize a cow.

I have grown personally attached to a small group of cows. These girls stay on the farm until it is clear that being alive is cumbersome and painful for them. When there seems to be no hope of any one of these girls ever recovering or being able to do something simple like stand up...I will end her suffering.

And it effing sucks. There is no other way to describe how it feels to put down a cow. In a cruel twist of bitter irony, the cows I am forced to put down are the same cows I feel the most affection toward. It just sucks.

It really, really sucks.

In case you're wondering, I do the deed in the most quick and painless way possible. I literally shoot the cow between the eyes.

My favorite cows die while staring at me.

I get emotional writing these words. I strongly remember the cows I have had to put down in the past. As I look ahead, I know some of my favorite girls will have to be put down in the future. It is a painfully raw action—which is why I will not outsource this act. I take responsibility for it. It's not fair to expect an employee to do this for me. I am the captain of this ship, and I will do the dirtiest work for my crew.

We humans have a precedent for this "taking of responsibility." You would not be responsible for pulling the plug of someone you have never met before. That unknown person might live halfway around the world, and as a result, is the responsibility of their own family. Instead, you would be responsible for making that decision for your mother or father. You have to make the hardest decisions in the world for the people who are the closest to you.

To be frank, I feel that taking responsibility and being there when I put down my cows is the most honorable way to end the life of these bright, wonderful animals. I want to be there; I want to have them feel the same connectedness we had shared throughout their life and to take that with them.

I hope that doesn't sound twisted to you. It is the exact same notion of being there to hold the paw of your own pet when the vet puts him or her to sleep. You want to feel the connection, but you also want your pet to feel relaxed and loved when they have the lights turned down…and then finally go out.

God knows, I hate even writing about this. I would imagine it has to be the same for veterinarians who euthanize animals. They can't love that part of their job. They do it because somebody has to. It's the right thing to do for a pet that can no longer live a life free from pain and suffering.

The same issue for a family member that has to stand by and honor a loved-one's living will. There could be something…some option or course of treatment…that might be done to continue your loved one's life. Medical science can keep people alive almost indefinitely these days. But your beloved relative has chosen to sign a DNR (Do Not Resuscitate). Meaning, he or she does not wish to be kept alive by artificial means. That person wants to be allowed to slip quietly into the night.

And somewhere, a family member is given the honor and the responsibility of allowing that to happen.

Is it necessary? Yes. The loved one might be in a coma and the doctors give them a zero percent chance of ever coming out of it.

Is it pleasant? No. I can't imagine having to live with the knowledge that you volunteered to end the life of a person you love so much. It is the right thing to do—and I would absolutely do it if I had to. But, it can't be easy.

Same thing with my girls.

Anyway, that's all I'm going to say.

It sucks.

Chapter 7
Sustainability: Whatever THAT Means

Farmers were the original environmentalists. You can't farm the same acreage for a hundred years or so without taking care of the land. We plant, we harvest, we plant again. In between, we take care of the soil.

These days, farmers have a lot of eco-jargon thrown at us by eco-activists.

"Organic" is the old, favorite standby. Once upon a time, that term just meant growing or producing food with only naturally-occurring fertilizers and pesticides (instead of synthetic ones). Activists were adamant that this was going to save the world, and the best way to do it was through…government regulation. Now, when you see that little green and white "organic" symbol on something in the store, it means a farmer spent a lot time filling out paperwork and spending too much money to get certified, only to end up with a low-yield crop that's not any healthier for you nor any better for the environment. But at least the consumer gets an expensive, low-quality product (Wilcox, 2011).

"Regenerative agriculture" is one of the newer buzzwords. Regenerative agriculture is the premise that degraded soils can be restored by keeping in mind how the soil is connected to water, plants, animals, and humans (Noble Research Institute, n.d.). However, there's no science behind any of the methods pertaining to this theory (Garnett & Godde, 2017).

"Sustainability" seems to be a favorite. It seems to be nothing more than a catch-all term for humans and nature existing in harmony—so that everybody benefits socially, economically, and environmentally (United States Environmental Protection Agency, n.d.). Could this possibly be a little more vague? This just sounds like…living life…in general.

These are just three of the countless number of eco-activist buzzwords out there. Each and every one of them are all based on farming practices that have been around for ages, yet everyone acts like we've never done them before. That's not to say older, more holistic methods are bad; often, they're just common sense. Somewhere along the way, though, activists decided that any sort of scientific advancement that made farming more efficient was wrong.

For example, activists would have you believe that using chemical fertilizers and pesticides are bad. These synthetic products don't take care of the soil naturally; they inhibit the soil from taking care of itself.

That is the attitude of a short-sighted and ignorant luddite. It's no different than refusing modern medical care. Should we give our kids an antibiotic to knock out their strep throat, or should we live "regeneratively" and allow the strep bacteria to live freely and multiply inside of our kid? After all, you're just allowing nature to take its course.

In other words, let's allow science to help our lives evolve naturally over time. I imagine you'd prefer travelling in your motor vehicle instead of travelling by covered wagon, right? I'm sure everyone would prefer painless dentistry to the barbaric practices of the 18th century. And you probably hit yourself with a little blast of DEET before you enter the woods on a camping trip.

Know what all those have in common? They are the result of technology advancing. When research develops a better mouse trap, the world is on fire to use it.

Fertilizers, pesticides, and plant modifications are all a part of the same advancements. They have been tweaked, changed, and perfected over time. They've been developed to the point where they don't impact the environment in a profoundly negative manner. We know more now than we did a hundred years ago. We have better products, better machines, and better protocols—and we use them to your advantage.

If the activists got their way 100% of the time, we'd be over-run by rats and insects, resulting in mass starvation in this country. The human population would be controlled by whatever resources would be left. Some food would grow (crops and livestock), but the amount would not sustain the population. Many humans would starve to death, or be killed outright for their resources.

I don't mean killed only by other humans. Think about it. If you and a bear are about to fight for a cache of food, you'd better have a gun. Otherwise, you lose that battle 100% of the time. Rats are numerous, tenacious, and clever. You'd better have some poison. Otherwise, you will lose that battle 100% of the time. Locusts multiply fast and swarm with almost no warning. You'd better have pesticides. Otherwise, you will lose that battle 100% of the time.

Not everyone is destined for survival in this model. The strong overpower the weak.

I didn't mean to get all dystopian on you. I want to drive home the point that dairy farmers are like everyone else. When the latest machine is invented, we take a look at it. If it can make our job easier, faster, or cheaper, we consider purchasing and using it. In the end, all of our savings (both time and money) get passed along to you, the consumer.

100

When we have to work harder, you end up paying a higher price for it. Ever wonder why a hurricane plowing through Florida will jack up the price of orange juice? It works the same with dairy.

More locally to Tillamook, a bunch of farmers started our Soil & Water Conservation District. We had no outside force that demanded we take care of our water and soil. We knew what to do. Proactive farmers worked together so these resources would be available for future generations.

I wanted to make sure to place those thoughts front-and-center. I'm tired of eco-activists dragging farmers in general, and dairy farmers specifically, over the coals, claiming we're destroying the Earth. They claim their arguments are rooted in science. But, as we all know, data can be manipulated and cherry-picked to "prove" an agenda.

The title of this chapter ("sustainability") refers to taking a word or concept and aligning the meaning to whatever is most convenient to the "cause" of a particular activist. It actually means what farmers take it to mean: cheap, abundant food that is available to everybody. Unfortunately, it too often means what activists twist it to mean: you must raise all food organically. Or to be more accurate, VE-ganically.

I believe these activists use the word "farmer" to apply to everybody; from large farms to your grandmother tending to her garden. They want to over-manage farming from the macro- to the micro-level. Their end game is to somehow have farmers produce all food without killing anything.

And I mean anything. For instance, not only should cows never be slaughtered, but no one should ever threaten the life of any other living thing. That goes right down to avoiding pesticides just because it may harm an insect. That means not keeping fields free from moles or voles because that would alter their life trajectory. That means not using commercial fertilizers, because that may threaten molds or fungi living in the soil.

In their minds, not only is this possible, but it makes perfect sense.

The evil farmers must be made to understand their negative impact on the planet and get behind the "proper" ideology. An ideology that was hatched by people who know nothing about farming.

Farming is like any other industry. Or individual. We live and learn and adjust along the way. At one time, factories were allowed to dump whatever toxic crap they produced into our water systems. That changed over time and with a little pressure from the EPA. Likewise, factories used to belch toxic gasses, smoke, and soot into the atmosphere. They also cleaned up over time and with a little pressure from the EPA.

Is this system perfect? No. By-products of production still seep into our world. Each industry is doing what it can to eliminate what it can, but the leftover waste is balanced against product production. We like our petroleum products, our rubbers and plastics, and our textiles. We enjoy the convenience of automobiles, air conditioning, and wood framing for our houses.

All of these comforts come at a cost. We understand the financial cost; everyone gets a monthly electric bill. But the environmental bill must also be considered. Trees are cut down, chemical by-products and wastes are produced, and landfills are heaped with mountains of refuse.

We strike a cost/benefit balance. It's a form of risk management.

Here is the reality in YOUR life: you do your best to keep the cost of your electric bill to a minimum. You may keep you home a little warmer in the summer and a little cooler in the winter; that way, you don't burn as much energy. Try as you might to convince others it's to "save the planet," we all know that it also comes down to money. Nobody wants a soaring electric bill.

In all honesty, if you really wanted to "save the planet," you would NEVER use air conditioning or heat. ALL of it comes at an environmental cost. You know damn good and well that it's not good for the planet. In fact, most of it is bad for the planet...but you cannot stand the thought of living in a world without heat or air conditioning. Therefore, you strike a balance. You do what you can to minimize the financial and environmental cost while you maximize the benefit of creature comforts.

All of us do it. We do it on a micro-level at home with our electric bills, and also with every other resource we consume. Factories and all manufacturing facilities do it on a macro-level by balancing profit with impact.

Yes, the bad apples exist. Some companies are run by idiots who don't give a crap about the world they leave behind. That's why we have government oversight. Not everyone will do the right thing if left to their own devices. That's why some oversight is necessary. But let's not allow the activists to grow drunk with power.

Balance, right?

Have a little perspective! Some companies are creating a toxic impact for reasons they don't even realize. Before "greenhouse gasses" were even a thing, Henry Ford had no idea his cars were coughing out carbon monoxide. Even if he did, there was no context within which to understand what that meant to the future of the world at large.

New information is discovered and gathered, and companies adjust accordingly. We can't reactively throw out the baby with the bath water.

When carbon monoxide output became an environmental and political talking point, change was initiated. But we did not abolish all internal combustion engines. When someone stood up and said, "Hey, these engines are putting poison into our air," we didn't rush to shut down Ford Motor Company and return to horses and buggies.

Instead, we set out to improve the product we already had. Engines became cleaner and more efficient. Emission systems became more robust. Testing began in urban settings so cars with broken or failing emission systems would get flagged and then repaired. Nobody burned the automotive empire to the ground. Smart people set out to solve the problem.

Eventually, electric vehicles will probably overtake the internal combustion vehicles. But once again, it is not immediate, nor without hiccups along the way. Believe it or not, electric cars have been around since the 1800s. In 1888, the Flocken Elektrowagen, designed by German inventor Andreas Flocken, was probably the world's first "real" electric car (Boyle, 2018). Believe it or not, that first electric car was only a couple years behind the first petroleum-powered car. Carl Benz commercially produced the first internal combustion engine automobiles in 1886 (Melosi, 2010).

Why did we go with ICE (internal combustion engine) instead of the electric car? It was a matter of cost and convenience. ICEs performed better and could be produced more inexpensively. Elon Musk brought battery technology to new heights and scaled production with his first model Tesla. But people didn't immediately rush to snatch them out of the showrooms like four-wheeled Cabbage Patch Kids. It took time to both improve the product and bring down the price. People wanted to know the electric cars would perform just as well as ICEs, have them cost the same or less, and create convenience.

Infrastructure takes time. We don't destroy ICEs and wait patiently for something better to come along. Instead, we do what we have always done; we tweaked an existing product to make it better until something superior was made.

How does this relate to dairy farming? The same concept does apply. Rather than completely destroy a thriving industry, we work to make it better. I'll share a brief blog post I wrote for Earth Day in 2021:

"...roughly 3.5 percent of all methane released globally comes naturally from the Amazon's trees," (Welch, 2021).

Without context, a narrative lacking real substance could spiral in any direction from this data point. Is the 3.5 percent a significant increase? Decrease? What contributed? How? Why?

Let's look at another one.

Agriculture represents only 9.9% of total US greenhouse gas emissions.

Can we move the needle?

We're doing our best, that's for sure.

The dairy industry, specifically, has reduced the carbon footprint of a single gallon of milk by 63 percent since 1944. We have become far more efficient.

Yet, we're often showcased as the worst offender to our planet's health.

It's funny, though, that while the world shut down because of the COVID pandemic, an emissions case study inadvertently took place. Planes, trains and automobiles halted, which account for 29 percent of greenhouse gas emissions (United States Environmental Protection Agency, 2021) and US emissions dropped by 10 percent.

And, this happened while cattle continued to consume plants and byproducts humans cannot digest using their unique digestive systems and transforming them into delicious, nutrient-rich products.

Now, let's add a layer.

Farmers and ranchers partner with programs like the Lesser Prairie-Chicken Initiative (Lesser Prairie Chicken Initiative, n.d.). This initiative strives to make up for the 11 million acres lost to development over the last 20 years by improving wildlife habitats — which then snowballs into improving the long-term sustainability of their land (Wernick, 2020).

What I'm saying here is it's not enough to take a viral meme or graphic at face value. Look beyond a single data point to see what's really happening.

I get it, though. Reading the EPA's 791 page U.S. Greenhouse gas emissions inventory report (United States Environmental Protection Agency, 2021) doesn't sound like the way I'd like to spend my afternoon either.

The good news, I'm going to continue showing and unfiltered, transparent insights in the food and

agricultural industries. And, if I'm not a subject-
matter expert, I'll find someone who can help answer
the
tough questions.

Happy Earth Day, friends.

All of my blogs can be found on my website, www.TDFHonest Farming.com.

When Don Schindler and his staff at DMI read that blog, they sent a nice email to me which included the following information:

As of 2007, producing a gallon of milk uses 90 percent less land and 65 percent less water, with a 63 percent smaller carbon footprint than in 1944, thanks to improvements made by dairy farmers in cow comfort, cow health and nutrition, and breeding.

In 2008, U.S. dairy was the first in the food agricultural sector to conduct a full life cycle assessment at a national level which showed it contributes just 2% of all U.S. greenhouse gas emissions. Thanks to increasingly modern and innovative dairy farming practices, the environmental impact of producing a gallon of milk in 2017 shrunk significantly, requiring 30% less water, 21% less land and a 19% smaller carbon footprint than it did in 2007 (personal correspondence).

In short, farmers are constantly trying to improve the quality of their product and the sustainability of our industry. We rely on the earth to provide the raw materials needed to do our job. Therefore, it makes no sense to destroy the hand that feeds us, so to speak.

It annoys me that this topic keeps getting thrown back at farmers. But rather than continue with broad generalities, let me give a few specific examples of how amazingly sustainable our industry has become.

First, my cows actually eat by-product waste from other industries. They are the ultimate recyclers. They eat canola meal, which is a by-product of the production of cooking oil and bio-diesel. Canola itself is an important crop from the standpoint of sustainability because it is grown in places where "normal" crops cannot grow. Put another way, canola grows well in places that human foods, or plants we can eat, cannot grow well.

If you've ever sped past a farm field blanketed by pretty yellow flowers, that's a field of canola. And here's a fun fact: canola is a product of farming science. It did not exist until the 1970s. It's actually a genetic hybrid of two types of rapeseed that were bred together using genetic science pioneered by Gregor Mendel, and extended by Canadian scientists at The University of Manitoba. Those scientists wanted a plant that produced an oil containing less erucic acid than the previous rapeseed plants (Wrigley, Corke, Seetharaman, and Faubion, 2016).

They developed the current iteration of this plant. The name "canola" comes from smashing together the words "Canada" (can) and an acronym for "oil, low acid" (ola).

Pretty cool, hey?

Canola is a robust plant that grows pretty much anywhere. It is planted in places that other crops wouldn't grow as well, thereby utilizing land that would otherwise be useless. The plant itself is important in a sustainable system. On a global economic scale, it is used in manufacturing fuel.

Diesel engines were originally developed in Germany by Rudolf Diesel, who, in 1893, unveiled a way to power an engine using vegetable oil. His original design utilized oil from a plant in the peanut family, arachis (Knothe, Krahl, and Gerpen, 2010). Nowadays, there are dozens of different plant oils used in the manufacturing biodiesel fuel. Because of the versatility and low cost of canola, it is often utilized for this purpose. Likewise, it is one of the most commonly available cooking oils.

When the oil is extracted from the canola plant, a grainy "meal" is left behind. My cows love canola meal. The cows also eat soy meal, a soy by-product similar to canola. Humans consume a tremendous amount of soy-based foods, so soy meal is another very common waste by-product.

I also feed cotton seeds to my cows. Cotton seeds are a by-product of cotton gins, which remove the seeds from the cotton during the production of textiles. Eight billion square yards of fabric are spun out of cotton each year (Cotton Counts, n.d.), and therefore tons of cotton seeds are removed and used as feed. The cows gobble it up, thereby consuming materials that would otherwise go to waste.

Let's return to canola for a specific example. Only about 44% of the canola plant is used to make oil (Canola Council of Canada, 2021), so well over half the harvest would have to be discarded, were it not for the fantastic ruminant digestive system in some farm animals, especially cows. Their stomach is uniquely designed to digest this type of material.

By "discarded" I mean that the seeds would probably get dumped into landfills. Those seeds would then ferment and give off carbon dioxide, thereby emitting greenhouse gases. Instead, they are eaten by cows, who turn the seeds into delicious dairy products.

In my part of the country, another byproduct is readily available and nutritious for my cows. It's called millrun, and is the by-product of milling flour. Like with biodiesel and textiles, milling flour creates waste. Rather than discarding it, we feed it to the cattle.

Not only do dairy farmers play a key role in sustainability via organic recycling, but we are instrumental in keeping consumer costs low. When we purchase cotton seeds, millrun, or canola meal from the companies that produce it, those same companies don't have to pay someone to discard or destroy the by-products. Thus, the companies make money from their garbage they would otherwise have to pay to get rid of. Their savings get passed along to the consumer. If the companies had to pay to discard those by-products, that cost would be added to the price of the product and paid by the consumer.

Get it?

As it pertains to dealing with larger corporations in general, I constantly shake my head and wonder why people don't understand basic economics. This is painfully evident when they start yelling about raising corporate taxes. Don't adults understand the way the world works anymore? A company's bottom line—the profits and losses—are not affected by raising taxes.

I have to say that again because I want everyone to allow this important fact to soak in: A company's bottom line—the profits and losses—are not affected by raising taxes.

A corporation won't feel the pain the same way you and I do because they won't lose money. They'll just raise the price of their products, and make YOU pay their higher taxes.

In reality, here are their three options—neither of which is ideal, and neither of which makes them pay "their fair share." Corporations never "pay" higher taxes; they either make consumers foot the bill (which nobody likes), they move out of state or overseas (which nobody likes), or else they go out of business and people lose a locally sourced product (which nobody likes).

Take a deep breath because what I am about to say is going to shock you: Other industries like to make money. Just like dairy farmers. There's that four-letter word—profit—again.

The agricultural by-products I mentioned earlier (like millrun) are the ones that are readily available in my part of the country. Depending upon your location, there might be other by-products that get purchased by livestock farmers and then fed to their animals. For example, farmers in Florida have access to tons of orange pulp. In California, farmers can purchase almond hulls, the "shell" around the nut. Beer breweries and liquor distilleries use a tremendous amount of grain which could be disposed of after they use it. Instead, nearby farmers use it as a protein-rich feed. Hang on to your hats: in eastern Pennsylvania—near the Hershey factory—cows get to eat chocolate!

Instead of throwing all these materials away, they're consumed.

My cows eat a mixed feed that contains silage—a mixture of corn, wheat, grain, or alfalfa that is harvested wet, covered, and then allowed to ferment. It also contains hay, which gets cut, dried by the sun, and then baled; and a combination of canola meal, soy meal, and cotton seed. Other additives are stirred in because our nutritionist recommends them, but pretty much 100% of my cows' diet consists of these ingredients.

Every morning, and then again every afternoon, my feed truck is filled with a combination of these materials. It mixes them into a grainy dish that keeps my girls happy and healthy.

***

Consuming waste products is only one branch of the dairy farm sustainability tree. I've already touched upon waste products created by the cows themselves (i.e., poop and pee). This waste makes a fantastic natural fertilizer. For small dairy farms, the farmers can apply the waste directly to their soil. It may not smell good while the farmer prepares the fields, but it is the ultimate act of recycling. The land produces the food, the cows eat the food, and the poop that results from the food gets fed back into the soil which then produces more food.

Larger operations have more options, and some of them are really cool. They use biodigesters (microbes, or bacteria) that break down the waste. Large dairy operations that produce hundreds of tons of waste every day send can that waste through a biodigester.

Ironically, the biodigester works almost identically to the rumen in a cow; it breaks down the poop in an anaerobic manner. This anaerobic digester creates methane gas, which can be burned as fuel. For example, it can be burned by a generator on the farm and then converted into electricity.

In case you're wondering, electricity isn't created by magic. It requires energy to create electricity. Wind turbines, which are basically propellers that are turned by the wind, create electricity (you can find them in fields of flat states, like Indiana). Water turbines, which are turned by passing water over them (like inside the Hoover Dam) create electricity. Nuclear plants, which use heat produced by nuclear fission, or decay (like at the Beaver Valley Nuclear Power Station, just outside of Pittsburgh, PA) create electricity. The heat turns water into steam, and the steam is condensed and used to turn turbines.

It's my understanding that those turbines have metal coils and wires in them, and when they are spun, static electricity is created and then captured for storage or usage. The alternator in your car is a perfect example of a small turbine. Gasoline is burned to create energy. That energy is converted into motion, thereby spinning the little turbine inside the alternator. That motion generates static electricity, which is then fed back into the battery or out to power the car's lights, computers, and dashboard.

Please, electrical engineers and automotive enthusiasts, don't get upset if I have a few of the details wrong. You get paid to know that stuff. I get paid to put cheese on your bologna sandwich.

Electricity is not produced out of thin air. It takes energy to make it. In fact, much of the electricity we use in our homes is generated through steam produced by burning fossil fuels (McLaren, 1984). That isn't a popular concept to discuss, but once again, there is no such thing as a free lunch.

On larger dairy farms, the cows can produce enough waste that all of the electricity for the operation comes from generators fueled by burning the methane that comes from poop and pee. The largest of these operations can actually make money off this process by selling some of their excess electricity back to the power company—who then redistributes, or sells, it to their customers.

Incidentally, the methane gas that results from digesting waste products doesn't have to be immediately burned off. It can also be liquefied and sold as liquid methane. In this form, it can be used for anything from heating your home or running your stove, all the way up to being refined and then combined with liquid oxygen to produce rocket fuel (Thunnissen, Guernsey, Baker, and Miyake, 2004).

As I have mentioned earlier, our farm isn't quite ready to add the infrastructure necessary to create electricity, but we will one day. Unfortunately, building the machinery to pull this off requires money (there's that doggone word again). We are just completing a large-scale upgrade to our facilities, and have chosen to make better living spaces for our cows before exploring options to generate electricity.

Just like your home, we have a budget. In keeping to the budget, we have to decide which expenses are necessary to pay first, and then which needs are prioritized to address with the money left over.

A digester is cool…but expensive.

***

Farms are not a drain on water (another pun; sorry). This is another topic that activists will harp about once in awhile, and they force me to confront them with reality.

They hate that.

However, before I defend dairy farming, I am going to point out the hypocrisy in this argument. As with many of these issues, I am consistently dismayed by the double-standard created by activists. When the pot calls the kettle black, it's time to clean up the whole kitchen.

They hate that even more.

Using water to keep crops healthy and dairy cattle hydrated is cited as an evil force dooming the world to depleted water resources. Let's compare this to a few basic human habits. People like to be clean. Heck, I like to be clean. Not as much as Kaycee wants me to be clean, but we're not too far apart with our expectations. Like most of this country's approximately 325 million residents, we take showers. Our kids take baths. Like many responsible people, we don't overdo it. Just about everyone bathes in some form or fashion, at least every day or every other day. That's a lot of grey water spiraling down the drain.

Next, let's look at suburban America. How many people water their lawns? Quite a few, actually. According to the EPA, landscape irrigation accounts for about one-third of all residential water use, amounting to over seven billion gallons per day (2008). A lot of water is reclaimed by the earth when the sprinkler jets water throughout the yard.

In fact, many cities, subdivisions, and businesses have their sprinkler systems set to automatic. The sprinkler system will kick on even when it's pouring down rain. That seems like insanity to me, but to each his own, I suppose. In any case, there's a lot of water wasted through this practice.

Lastly, let me throw in an element of human living that is completely gratuitous: swimming pools. Listen, I get it. When compared to the amount of water used to clean humans and water their lawns, the amount put into swimming pools is definitely way lower. However, it is another shining example of how flippant people can be when they are part of the problem. It's much easier to point a finger at someone else than it is to alter one's own lifestyle.

Yet, how are dairy farms not a part of the water issue?

This topic probably affects me less than farmers in some of the drier parts of the country. I live in northwest Oregon, which gets ample rainfall and has moderate temperatures, leading to low evaporation throughout the year. The Wilson River runs full, our pond remains high, and we pay for city water for our cows to drink. Obviously these variables can fluctuate during wetter and drier months, but on average, we are overall flush with water (another pun—I can't help it).

As for other dairy farmers, we "recycle" water at least three times.

First, all dairy farms have a simple device called a plate cooler. A plate cooler acts like a radiator; it's designed to cool the milk before it's put into refrigeration. Water-cooled tubes run through the milk, thereby absorbing a lot of the milk's heat and transferring it to the water.

Incidentally, when milk comes out of a cow, it comes out at 101 degrees Fahrenheit (38.3 degrees Celsius). The milk is run through the plate cooler, which takes its temperature down to 50-60 degrees Fahrenheit (10 to 15.5 degrees Celsius).From there, milk goes to refrigeration, which takes the temperature down further, thereby creating one component of keeping the milk fresh.

The plate cooler allows us to burn less energy in our refrigeration units. It takes over half the heat out of the milk before we send the milk to refrigeration. Because the milk isn't as warm, it requires less electricity to cool it down to a safe temperature.

The warm water from the plate cooler is then deposited into the water troughs where the cows drink it. The cows prefer the warmer water—it's easier for them to tolerate than cold water. It's a win/win.

The water then runs through the cow. I don't think I need to explain this one. When it exits the cow, it's captured and—along with poop—gets spread back onto the fields in the form of fertilizer.

So yes, cows and milk require water. But, we do everything we can to recycle and remain as sustainable as possible. We probably do it better than most humans, to be honest.

***

These are three prime examples (consuming waste by-products, recycling cow waste into energy, and recycling water) of how dairy farming is completely in step with the current ideology about recycling and sustainability. In fairness, most people don't think much about water, feed, or energy. However, most people are at least casually acquainted with the notion of cow farts. We are all told ad infinitum about cow farts shooting methane gas into the atmosphere. Let me break this notion down.

First of all, I hate that the conversation in popular media is so heavily focused on greenhouse gas emissions. It completely overlooks the fact that we are doing a fabulous job of being sustainable. As an industry, we are so much farther ahead of where we were even 30 years ago. Instead, the media and the public get lost in the distorted minutia of cow flatulence.

Who gets hurt by all of this lunacy? The little guy, of course.

Our country beats its chest daily about how we want to "look out for the little guy" and "save Joe Lunchbox." But every new regulation, rule, tax, and test the government puts out (as they bow to pressure from activists) forces farmers to either purchase new equipment or change what they are doing to a less efficient procedure. Unlike most corporations that produce a product, such as car companies, shoe manufacturers, and breakfast cereal makers, we can't simply raise our prices to reflect our increased overhead.

What happens if a large shoe manufacturer gets hit with a fine or a new tax or a new regulation that forces them to build a new, greener factory? They bump the price of their shoes a dollar or two per pair.

They don't lose money. You do!

However, the price of milk is fixed. Ironically, that fixed price is determined by the same government forcing new regulations. A cow can only produce so much milk, and a farmer can only sell that finite amount of milk for the "allowed" amount. There's no "wiggle room."

Larger farms have the financial stability to compensate. They can adjust and absorb the hit. They can add a few cows or fire an employee to counteract the financial loss created by the regulations. Smaller farms operate too close to the margins. They cannot simply snap their fingers and magically make new infrastructure appear out of thin air. It all costs money—that ugly concept that keeps popping up.

When activists pressure the media to act as magicians by tantalizing the public with frenetic complaining over greenhouse gasses and cows, the focus is diverted from the real problem. Nobody wants to hear it, but: Dairy farming represents only a tiny fraction of the problems related to greenhouse gasses. And I have a man of science to back me up.

I have a lot of respect for Frank Mitloehner, a professor at the University of California at Davis. He has spent his career working toward establishing environmentally benign livestock systems. He consults with farmers to help them minimize the environmental impact of their business.

In an article published online by Dairy Management, Inc. (DMI), whose website I highly recommend (www.usdairy.com), Frank is also confused as to why the dairy industry gets no recognition for progress. He says, "We have seen changes in the U.S. dairy industry that are astounding,…They are the envy of the world, but for whatever reason they are painfully quiet about it,"("Can dairy," 2021).

I'm guessing he wasn't referring to my social media accounts. "Quiet" doesn't suit me. Thank goodness for my wife—she keeps me in check. I can't imagine what my Facebook videos would look like if she didn't keep me reigned in. I would love to create a separate book to just rant about politics.

Again, I digress.

Frank goes on to mention that the dairy industry is not the major cause of greenhouse gases. He cites data published by the EPA (Environmental Protection Agency) that says there are three sectors that produce nearly 80% of all greenhouse gas emissions in the U.S.: transportation, power production, and industries ("Can dairy," 2021). I am in 100% agreement on this.

Let me break that down for you: cars, electricity, and manufacturing.

We love our cars in America. We love our air conditioning and smart phones in America. We love our carpeting, ball caps, and take-out food. The activists and environmentalists go after these industries, too. They are at least consistent, and they have no doubt made the world a cleaner place to live in. I give them credit for that. But I wonder why they constantly beat the drum of cow farts. As Frank mentions in the article, the EPA found that all species of livestock produce only 4% of all greenhouse gasses.

Four. Percent.

All of this hubbub is whipped up to make everyday folks believe that cows are responsible for destroying the ozone and bringing an end to civilization as we know it. You wanna bring about real environmental change? Go back to the stone age! Let's eliminate all motorized vehicles and ride horses everywhere (horses fart too, by the way). Let's stop producing electricity and burn torches to find our way at night. And let's stop manufacturing all the creature comforts we have come to enjoy.

All except for Cream Cheese Danishes at Lindsey's Lattes in Tillamook. I'm not sure I could live without those.

Frank concludes by saying, "...there are people out there who will claim there is nothing worse and more environmentally detrimental than the livestock sector. That clearly is not supported by science," ("Can dairy," 2021).

So what's the deal?

That level of misdirection has a purpose. The Forces That Be want you to dislike dairy farming, so they divert your focus away from the overwhelming positives in our industry. Attention is turned toward the one negative they can exploit. The funny thing is, cow farts (or, more scientifically, bovine methane emissions) really aren't a huge issue when compared to the global, big picture issue.

While we're looking at the big picture, let's not forget that larger populations are responsible for larger portions of the problem. Lest we forget, China, India, and Europe all have massive numbers of people, yet fewer EPA-like restrictions. They account for a far larger percentage of the greenhouse gas issue.

I get it. Change begins at home. The U.S. is where we live, so let's do what we can to clean up our own backyard.

My farm is categorized as a CAFO (Concentrated Animal Feeding Operation). I am watched by a couple agencies, both governmental and private, that make sure I adhere to rules and regulations designed to protect the environment. I have to have a nutrient management plan, pay attention to where I apply manure, keep track of records for auditing purposes, and make myself a better farmer.

According to DMI, there are 31,000 dairy farms and farm families in the United States ("Can dairy," 2021). That's a lot of individual pieces weaving together to create the tapestry of our industry. Every one of those farms is more sustainable than the generation before it. Let's not throw out the baby with the bathwater. We're doing a damn good job keeping up with the changing needs of the world around us.

***

This issue of cows farting has become a bit of a punch line... and why not? The concept appeals to the 13-year-old boy humor in me. Once again, it's not even a cause for concern. Yes, cows fart; so did my grandmother, but I don't think I need to share stories of that, either. However, allow me to clear the air (pardon the pun—I'm out of control with these things) and return to rumen and Biology 101.

Everyone farts because of the fermentation taking place in their gut. Depending on your specific biology, certain foods interact with our natural gut microbes and ferment at different speeds. Lactose intolerant people bloat and fart like a hot air balloon if they drink a milkshake. Conversely, other people can down a five-pound block of cheese and pass it like traffic on the freeway. In humans, fermentation takes place deep in the gut, so the most efficient egress for the gases to escape is via the anus.

That sounded so polite. I'm kind of proud of that last paragraph.

When cows ingest food, fermentation takes place in their rumen. Therefore, the methane gases created through this process are more likely belched out than farted out. Cows do fart, but the primary methane producer is their rumen, thereby making them belch way more than they fart.

I'm pretty sure my teenage son is giggling hysterically as he reads this segment.

Furthermore, Frank Mitloehner also mentioned that, from a long-term perspective, methane isn't nearly as impactful as carbon dioxide. Methane has a lifespan of about 12 years. It is released, and then over the next decade or so, breaks down through the process of oxidation. Carbon dioxide, on the other hand, has a lifespan of nearly 1,000 years before it is broken down and eliminated ("Can dairy," 2021).

Twelve years may seem like a long time. Yet, cows have been around for longer than twelve years, right? Thus, every molecule of methane that is produced and released today is merely replacing a molecule that was released twelve years ago. Because the one released twelve years ago has subsequently been eliminated by way of oxidation ("Can dairy," 2021).

As a result, no new methane is added to the system. It's like five kids lined up and jammed on a couch. When a new kid shoves his way onto the couch, a kid already there gets knocked off the end. The new kid replaces one of the current kids. The couch still holds five kids, and that's all it will hold.

However, motor vehicles have not been around for 1,000 years. So with every new molecule of carbon dioxide your Ford or Chevy pushes into the air, it joins the blanket of carbon dioxide already hovering in the atmosphere. They're all going to be there for centuries, doing their thing to trap in heat from solar radiation. That is pretty scary.

Let's at least focus our efforts to clean up an industry that leads the pack when it comes to environmental issues. Leave the dairy farmers alone. Their herds can eat, burp, and produce the dairy products that help your kids grow strong bones and teeth.

Chapter 8
A Day in the Life of Milk

Milk is probably the freshest product you can find in a grocery store. Because it can spoil so quickly, it is also one of the most regulated products you will find at your local grocery store. It goes through several steps to ensure its freshness and purity.

Most times, less than two days have elapsed between the time a cow gets milked to the time you pour the milk into your glass at home. The supply chains we have created in the United States are phenomenally efficient. They run like a well-oiled machine to make sure you get the best and safest product in the timeliest manner.

So what is that journey like? And what are the safety procedures we take to make sure nobody gets sick from the milk?

Glad you asked….

***

Obviously, milk is produced in a cow's udder. Udders are like breasts in human females; they exist solely to produce the milk needed to nourish a newborn. Talking through udder development, milk formation, and all of the hormones involved is a little above my pay grade. I don't interact with the udder until the milk has already been produced by the cow; so, let's begin the journey there.

This is probably the part of my job that is most fascinating to everyone who tours our facilities. To be milked, cows are led into our milking parlor. As they enter, they are placed on a rotating platform that allows them to comfortably stand and eat while they are being milked. The platform rotates slowly, allowing for a cow to enter an open slot, get milked, and then walk off the other side. Their vacated slot then rotates to the next cow in line, who steps on to be milked next.

Lather, rinse, repeat.

In the old days, the farmer would have to take a knee next to the cow and milk her by hand. If you've seen that on television, it looks fairly simple. Skilled farmers develop their technique, and can empty an udder pretty quickly. However, if you have ever tried to milk a cow at a state fair (for example) you'll find it isn't as easy as it looks. Or, should I say, it isn't easy if you don't know the technique. I won't bore you with the details; I'm sure there are a slew of YouTube videos on the topic. Suffice it to say, we have moved on to using machines to do the milking for us.

Honestly, the machines are also better for the cows. The suction cups placed over the nipples (teats) are more sanitary and more comfortable for the cow than if they were to get milked by hand, even by a farmer who knows what he's doing.

The machines use suction, which can irritate the teats over time. Each cow is treated with a balm to help salve chapped teats and also to prevent disease. As I have mentioned earlier, mastitis is quite uncomfortable, and would be quite common without the treatments for the cows. Several products exist to treat the teats post-milking. The balm is poured into a cup—into which each teat is dipped, one after the other. The balm soothes chafed skin and crates a barrier against infection.

The milk exits the cow at 101.5 degrees Fahrenheit. It immediately gets cooled to 50 or 60 degrees by the plate cooler. The milk is then transferred to refrigeration storage, where it awaits the daily truck that comes around to transport the milk to the milk plant.

The milk from any cow that is on a regimen of antibiotics is kept separate from the rest of the milk. I know some people are concerned that farmers might proactively keep their cows on prophylactic antibiotics. A lot of buzz goes around about farmers adding antibiotics to the cows' feed or pumping them full of antibiotics to prevent infection.

Let me put your concerns to rest: I cannot think of a dumber idea.

I don't know if every farmer across the country (or the world) has a ton of knowledge about antibiotic resistance, but I'm sure they have many thoughts about their bottom line. It would make no sense financially to invest the amount of money required to keep the cows pumped full of antibiotics every day of their lives. And to put a fine point on it, it is far more cost effective to structure the cows' lives in a healthy way.

An ounce of prevention is worth a pound of cure, right?

We all consult regularly with nutritionists and veterinarians. There isn't a vet alive that would recommend medicating a healthy cow, despite antibiotic resistance. Yes, organic farmers are more conservative in their approach to antibiotic resistance. They are required to do so. As for me, I don't want my girls to suffer through a protracted illness of bacterial infection. When they are sick, I ensure they are nursed back to health.

Again, I cannot speak for all 31,000 dairy farms in the U.S. Bad farmers are out there, just like bad activists, bad politicians, and bad bankers. But I will absolutely tell you this: At our farm, we do no such thing. We only give medication if the cow is sick. End of story.

Because the antibiotics will cross into a cow's udders, and therefore contaminate her milk supply, her milk gets discarded if she is taking medicine. For all the other cows, their milk finds its way onto the milk truck.

***

An insulated tanker truck shows up at our farm twice per day. The driver takes the milk from each milking separately. Smaller farms might only have one milk truck per day, but never less than that. Milk doesn't stand still for very long at any location.

The driver of the milk truck takes a sample of the milk. Once the milk is delivered to the milk plant, another sample is taken. Both samples are tested to ensure the purity and the overall health rating of the milk. As I said, milk is one of the most regulated foods at the supermarket.

If any of the standards set by the FDA are not met, all the milk from that batch is discarded. The government doesn't mess around when it comes to protecting consumers from bad food.

After arriving at the milk plant and testing the batch, the milk is immediately standardized. The process of standardization in this context means that the cream is separated from the skimmed milk; it is skimmed off the top.

They do this because they can then add the cream (also called the milk fat) back in at different percentage levels. Milk is never watered down, despite what you may read on the internet. And you all know what I think about things on the internet.

Always check the source, people. Always check the damn source.

When you were a kid, I'll bet you thought of milk as just milk. So did most people for a long time. It wasn't until 1980 when the USDA published their first dietary guidelines did anyone start thinking about the fat content in milk (Green, 2013). As our country grew more and more health conscious (we pay attention to science and technology), the percentage of fat in milk became more prominent in a consumer's purchasing decision.

Whole milk is defined as milk with 3.5 percent fat content, as determined by weight. Once again, we don't use volume as our measuring stick; we use weight. To make things simple, every one hundred pounds of whole milk must include 3.5 pounds of fat. Not surprisingly, 2% milk contains two percent fat by weight; 1% milk contains one percent by weight; skim contains no fat.

Make sense?

Because very few, if any, people think like this when they purchase milk, here is a more useful breakdown:

Whole milk has 8 grams of fat, and 150 calories per 8 ounce serving.

2% milk has 5 grams of fat and 120 calories per 8 ounce serving.

1% milk has 2.5 grams (100 calories).

Skim is basically fat-free (80 calories).

Interestingly, there are several nutritional factors that remain steady, regardless of which milk you buy. For example, it doesn't matter which percentage of milk you have in your fridge. In every eight ounce serving, all milk contains about 30% of the USRDA (Unites States Recommended Daily Allowance) of calcium, and consistent levels of seven other essential nutrients, like Vitamins A and D, Vitamin B12, and niacin (What do milk fat percentages mean?, 2018). The only difference is the fat and calories…and the taste.

For me, I need to experience the full flavor of milk. Milk should be mildly sweet, enhanced by the fat content. I grew up drinking whole milk straight from our tank, so I am perhaps a bit biased and spoiled. I don't care for skim milk because it just doesn't taste like milk to me. I understand that many people need to cut fat and calories in their diet, but I still don't like it.

***

At the milk plant, the milk remains cold. It is always refrigerated at 40 degrees Fahrenheit (4.44 degrees Celsius) or below. The only exception to this rule can happen after the milk gets pasteurized, which also happens at the milk plant.

Many foods get pasteurized, as I have previously mentioned. This is the process in which food is heated until many bad bacteria are killed and removed. The process, famously invented in the 1860s by its namesake, Louis Pasteur, is efficient in eliminating nasty bacteria like Staphylococcus, Listeria, and Salmonella, among others (Pearce et al., 2012).

Milk has a few different methods of pasteurization. For low temperature (also known as Vat or batch) pasteurization, the milk is held at 145 degrees Fahrenheit (63 degrees Celsius) for 30 minutes. This method works best to remove harmful bacteria, but to also retain the taste and texture of the milk. Most milk plants use this method to churn out the best tasting and safest product possible (Zahidul, 2020).

The second method is HTST, which is probably the most common technique. The acronym stands for "High Temperature, Short Time." Executing this method requires the milk be heated to 161 degrees Fahrenheit (72 degrees Celsius) for 15 seconds. People who own a small handful of cows and milk mostly for their own consumption will generally opt for this method. It is faster, and does not require either constant monitoring or specialized equipment (Zahidul, 2020).

Lastly, there is also ultra-high-temperature pasteurization. This method is for milk that you'll find on store shelves instead of in the refrigeration section. Using this method, the milk gets super-heated to 280 degrees Fahrenheit (138 degrees Celsius), and then held there for a mere two seconds. This method is ostensibly impossible to pull off in a private residence, as special equipment is absolutely necessary (Zahidul, 2020).

The pasteurized milk created through this process is immediately placed into a sealed container, and will not require refrigeration until it is opened. Most of this milk can remain safe to drink for up to nine months prior to opening. For milk pasteurized by either Vat or HTST, the product can last for around two weeks, if refrigerated at 40 degrees Fahrenheit or below, before it goes bad.

***

After standardization and pasteurization, the milk fats are added back to create the different types of milk. Vitamins A and D are also added, as those naturally occurring nutrients are fortified in line with government dietary guidelines that are supposed to improve the health of our nation. Similar to how some drinking water is infused with small amounts of fluoride to give our country better teeth (I know this is a controversial issue, but that doesn't mean it isn't happening).

Next, homogenization takes place. As I wrote earlier, homogenization is when the fats are broken up so they remain suspended in the milk. The milk gets squirted through a fine filter at extremely high pressure. Rather than having the cream separate from the skim, the level of fat and flavor throughout the entire jug remains consistent. Much like how Kellogg's somehow figured out a way to keep raisins suspended in Raisin Bran cereal.

Why aren't they all settled at the bottom of the box? I still haven't figured this out.

Milk that is pasteurized may not always be homogenized. However, that is far less likely and doesn't make a lot of sense. For advocates of milk "the old fashioned way," pasteurization eliminates most health risks, but leaving the milk unhomogenized can maintain the integrity of the milk/cream relationship.

Lastly, the milk is sent to the packaging wing of the milk plant. Here, it is run through machines that marry milk with container. Jugs, cartons, and boxes of all shapes, colors, and sizes can be used, depending upon the type and the brand of milk. Nearly 100% of this process is automated. In terms of measurement and waste, machines are more cost-effective because they are faster and more accurate than humans could ever be.

Once packaged and stacked, the milk is loaded almost immediately onto refrigerated 18-wheelers for distribution to the different milk outlets. Larger grocery stores and bigger discount chains (Wal-Mart and Costco, for example) will get at least one truck full of fresh milk straight from the milk plant each morning. Smaller outlets like gas stations, convenience stores, and rural markets might receive their milk from a middle-man that distributes milk from a centralized warehouse facility.

***

Your grocer rotates the available milk so that the older milk is displayed toward the front of the cooler. Their goal is to sell the milk and not have to discard it, resulting in lost profits (that four letter word again). So they want people to purchase the milk in the same order by which it was received at the store. Monday milk should sell before Tuesday milk, and so on.

Customers often try to outsmart the system and grab a fresher jug form the back of the pile, thereby leaving the older jugs to languish toward the front. But rest assured, the expiration dates are merely guidelines for the grocer. The date is also a conservative approach; if you drink some milk that is a day or two past its "sell by" date stamped on the carton, you should be fine.

In my experience, grocers are pretty good at knowing exactly how much milk to order for their customer base. There is very little milk that ultimately gets wasted. From a commercial standpoint, milk is a solid staple in the diet of most Americans.

In the end, you grab a jug of milk, toss it into your shopping cart, and then take it home to enjoy.

And that's the journey of milk, from cow to table.

Chapter 9
Dumping the Raw CAFOs, or Something Like That

I grew up on raw milk. Our family drank from the tank, which means we drew our milk from our milk supply before the insulated tanker truck came and took it to the plant for processing. Pretty much from the cow to our table, with a little bit of cooling in the meantime.

That's what "raw milk" is. There are no steps (with the exception of cooling) between the udder and your table. No standardization. No pasteurization. No homogenization. Udder to bottle to fridge.

I still drink it this way and I absolutely love the taste and texture. It's the best way to drink milk, in my opinion. However—and this is an important point—I would not sell it to anyone. That's right. I drink it, still to this day, but wouldn't sell it. I don't have any problem with consuming raw milk, or with the farmers doing what they can to make a buck or two. As long as you're not treading into my territory, I don't judge how you run yours.

I need to clarify that "raw milk" and "organic milk" are very different terms. There is a lot of overlap between organic farmers and farmers who sell raw milk. However, the term "organic" is protected; it is clearly defined and strictly regulated by the USDA.

Like many bureaucratic and legal endeavors put together by the government, the regulations fill an entire binder. A farm has to apply to be certified organic. Once accepted, they are regularly inspected and audited to make sure they maintain the practices set forth by the certification.

The government has strict, clear guidelines for any products or farms producing the products that are to be certified "organic" by the National Organic Program. This program was established by the Secretary of Agriculture in 1990 (Agricultural Marketing Services, 2020). The reams of information can be summarized thusly:

"Organic" is a labeling term for food or agricultural products ("food, feed or fiber") that have been produced according to USDA organic regulations, which define standards that "integrate cultural, biological, and mechanical practices that foster cycling of resources, promote ecological balance, and conserve biodiversity," (Agricultural Marketing Services, 2020).

Organic milk sold in your local market is still pasteurized and homogenized, just like any of the milk sold in the same sections of the cooler. The only difference between them is the difference in certification and regulation standards.

I grow a little uneasy when I hear about the uptick in raw milk sales. I'm not being pejorative when I use the phrase "raw milk," but a couple of issues immediately spring to mind when I hear about raw milk sold on roadside stands and other places. Wilsonview, my farm, is not a certified organic farm. Likewise, we do not sell raw milk.

The raw milk movement is still in its infancy. There are no major chain grocery stores picking it up, nor is there widespread penetration into the milk market as of yet. This is probably with good reason—a grocer would take on a lot of liability if their stores were to carry raw milk.

First, there isn't an organization that oversees the production and distribution of raw milk, so it's hard to judge the quality of the product. I know I've said it a couple times before, but milk is one of the most regulated food products in the United States. However, raw milk falls off this radar because it is still somewhat of an underground product. Raw milk farmers don't sell their milk to grocery chains, so the milk does not have to go through testing and quality control protocols.

That still isn't the kiss of death, but I am of the opinion (and this is only my opinion) that the milk I drink from our tank has a higher probability of being "clean" than milk from a small, raw milk farmer. In this instance, the word "clean" means that my milk probably has less bacteria and lower somatic cell counts than the raw milk farmer's milk.

I know of several really good raw milk farmers who do a fine job adhering to the closely-regulated "organic" standards of keeping their herd and their milk clean. They do well in controlling somatic cell counts. Yet, I am wary because the philosophy of pure organic farming leaves open the possibility of microbial infections getting transferred to humans.

If a farmer truly abides by the organic standards (as many raw milk farmers do), he or she is averse to giving antibiotics of any form to their cows at any time. They have their herd fight through infections rather than medicate them.

Again, I understand the philosophy. It's about allowing the immune system to do its thing and develop its own strength and strategy to combat the infection. Some people subscribe to the same philosophy. If their child contracts an ear infection, they use homeopathic remedies, or possibly allow the infection to "run its course" without antibiotic treatment.

In general, this could work. To reiterate my opinion on life choices, I don't judge other people's decisions. I live in a country where adults are free to manage their lives as they see fit, intervening only when that person transgresses into my or my family's life.

On the other hand, I prefer to shorten the duration and intensity of my children's discomfort, so Kaycee and I opt to seek the advice of a pediatrician when our kids get ear infections. We have no problem medicating when we and the physician feel it's appropriate and medically necessary.

We similarly medicate our cows when they have an infection—mastitis being the most prominent example. Cow falls ill, we give medicine, cow gets better. Fairly simple equation. Organic farmers will potentially allow infections to run their course, thereby increasing the possibility of low-grade infections hanging around for a while. A cow may fall ill, be appropriately separated from the herd, and recover enough to rejoin the herd. However, she may not have completely kicked the infection, so a few bad bacteria might be hanging around and find its way into her milk.

I'm not saying this does happen; I'm saying it could happen. And it makes me uneasy.

The second issue that springs to mind is that the raw milk I drink from the tank comes from cows that live, eat, and breathe in the same place I do. My family and I are exposed to the same allergens, toxins, bacteria, and environmental agents as the cows. If there is something bad that finds its way from cow to milk, my body has probably already developed a natural immunity to it. My immune system has acclimated to the exact same environment as my cows' bodies. We jibe, from that standpoint.

I have no supporting data, and there is probably very little scientific merit to my claim. But it makes common sense to me. And I am nothing, if not commonly sensical.

A raw milk farmer and his or her family may also drink happily and healthily from their own tank. But, if that same raw milk farmer sells their milk to a tourist from out of the area, the tourist and the cows are not being raised in the same environment. The tourist has a higher possibility of being affected by the different microorganisms in the milk.

Again, I believe that these farmers should have the right to produce and sell raw milk. Likewise, I hope the folks purchasing and consuming that milk are making informed decisions. Even I have toyed with the idea of selling pre-homogenized milk from our farm. It's all good with me. However, I would not sell the raw, unpasteurized milk.

I don't want to assume that risk. So many milk-borne illnesses and historical examples of disease outbreaks have been brought about by raw milk, that I would prefer to minimize risk and pasteurize my milk before selling it. Pasteurization wipes out so many issues that it seems prudent to do with all milk sold off a farm.

Smaller farms have a niche product with their milk. The raw movement has allowed a number of them to make money without having to deal with the commercial milk market. They can make a decent living by milking 20-100 cows using this approach. More power to them, seriously. The raw milkers sell a great tasting product that most consumers would never get a chance to experience if they didn't grow up around dairy cows. But, if you ask me, I would advise the buyer to pasteurize that milk before serving. The milk doesn't have to be homogenized; the sweet layer of cream is delectable.

I think you all know how much I love milk. Aside from it providing my income, I think it is also remarkably nutritious, it tastes great, and it is the chief ingredient in so many yummy foods, such as cheese, ice cream, and so on. I also love the industry and often welcome visitors to tour our farm. Once I get financially stabilized following this big expansion we have been undergoing (for what seems like forever), I am going to build and open a Visitor Center on our farm. That way, tourists can have a centralized site to assemble, get more information, have questions answered, and sample our product.

But—and this is a big but—I am only planning to serve coffee and ice cream in the Visitor Center. That decision might change by the time you read this book, but for now, I want to minimize risk. Even if I did serve milk samples, it would be pasteurized and homogenized milk. No way would I serve raw milk to tourists.

People have a number of allergies and reactions to milk. Their decision to purchase and/or drink milk is between them and their doctor. Ice cream is about as safe as we can be with regard to risk.

And who doesn't love ice cream?

That's my story, and I'm sticking to it.

***

Occasionally, videos appear online and circulate through social media platforms about milk dumping. The videos may depict someone talking about "farmers they know" who are paid by the U.S. government to dump their milk, destroy their crops, or just not produce any food at all. Or, the video may show actual video footage of tanker trucks dumping milk into a field.

If you have neither seen nor heard of these videos, then good for you. Stay the course.

These videos imply that the government is attempting to create a food shortage. In reality, the videos and the related messaging are meant to incite panic among citizens. The endgame of whomever lies behind this ideology is nefarious; no two ways about it.

I've said numerous times on my social media feeds that farmers in the U.S. do not sell their products (whether they be dairy, meat, or crops) to the government. We sell to private industry. No scenario in a rational universe exists where somebody could "know a guy" who got a letter from the U.S. government telling a farmer they would get paid to destroy the food they worked hard to produce.

End of story.

There is no way the United States government—or any government, for that matter—would ever destroy food to force a food shortage. Even a Communist government would want farmers to produce the food, but then the government would rather control it instead of destroy it.

Destroying food makes no sense; hungry citizens do violent things. The breakdown in social order and the sheer chaos that followed Hurricane Katrina in 2005 illustrates this perfectly. Hungry citizens of New Orleans, desperate for food and water, devolved into a hunter/gatherer state. We are generally a polite and communal society in the United States. But amid a crisis of that proportion, a person's center of focus narrows to themselves and their family. As the crisis continues, eventually the strong overpower the weak.

If you take a historical perspective, many major revolutions around the globe were triggered by food shortages in conjunction with grotesquely inflated food prices. People will put up with a lot of crap from despotic rulers, but screw around with their food, and citizens will revolt.

Be they elected or elevated by force, the ruling class wants to maintain control. They aim to control the citizens by controlling basic needs, such as food. They don't want a revolution; they want compliance, peace, and quiet.

With regard to the second point, the video footage of milk dumping is real. However, it is not happening in the United States. The videos are circulated with the implication that it is happening in your backyard, but that's not true. The footage comes from countries where farmers have no market within which to sell their milk—and their farms are dying as a result. When the economy crashes, the markets collapse. Farmers are then forced to discard perishable products.

**

The acronym CAFO stands for "Concentrated Animal Feeding Operation." It is a term used in propaganda videos and social media posts to throw hate at farms that milk and feed their cows in a barn rather than on an open range.

Sounds pretty horrific, right?

This segment could have easily found its way into the chapter on sustainability because it has to do directly with water conservation. Frankly, it could have found its way into several different chapters because it is one of the many topics that irritate me. The lies, misinformation, and preying the activists do upon their uninformed and highly emotional audience really infuriates me.

The acronym CAFO itself is used to demonize livestock farmers in general. Often, it's aimed at dairy farmers because of the way we milk and feed our animals. Cows can eat grasses under the sky, and farmers can milk them using mobile milking parlors. Neither approach is perfect; in fact, they are largely dependent upon the weather in the farm's part of the world. For example, winter snow means no natural grass to eat during that time of the year. I live in Oregon. You can put two and two together from there.

Typically, you'll see CAFO used interchangeably with the phrase "factory farm" to imply that bigger dairy farmers treat their cattle like faceless chattel. They're thought of as just pieces and parts moving on a big conveyor belt of the evil corporate empire. When a piece or part breaks, you throw it away and replace it with another piece.

No standard, exact definition of a "factory farm" exists. In my humble opinion, a factory farm could be "any size farm you don't happen to like." The term sounds hauntingly Orwellian, so it serves the agenda of furthering a narrative. On a factory farm, these are not animals; they're just things that are owned and exploited for all they're worth.

The assumption made by activists (and demonstrated thematically by several of the topics in this book) is that automation makes the farmers care less about their cows. The truth of the matter is, automation actually makes it easier to care for the needs of the cows. For instance, if you have an automatic scraper that cleans the waste out of a barn, two good things happen. First, the cows have a cleaner, safer barn where they can eat and relax. Second, the farmer has more time because they doesn't have to manually scrape cow poop several times per day.

I have to give another example, because we are pretty excited about getting these on the farm. Electronic Activity Monitors are collars our cows will wear when our systems upgrade is complete. These collars collect data about the cows' activity, which will provide useful information, like when a cow goes into heat. When she enters heat, she becomes a lot more active, thereby leading to a spike in her activity records. The data is automatically uploaded into our system when the cows enter the milking parlor. This awesome device will prevent us from missing the early signs of estrus.

Conversely, the activity monitor will alert us if a cow's activity drops steeply. In these instances, the cow may have fallen ill or may have been injured. Once again, this eliminates the potential of human error. It's nigh impossible to overlook the alerts or the data. However, without the alerts, we could possibly not notice if a cow is feeling sick.

Every time a cow gets milked, we get 12 hours of data downloaded into the system. We set the system up to alert us when a cow goes beyond

128

certain parameters (i.e., she's more or less active). Technology is our friend.

The more efficient the process, the more time a farmer has. That time can then be used to tend to sick cows, help fresh cows, and notice when a cow is acting unusual and may need attention. We'll also get the time to keep up with infrastructure (like, fix leaky barn roofs, mix feed thoroughly, mend fences, scare off predators, etc.) so it will all stay in tip-top shape.

This new tech makes sense to me. Or, maybe I'm just a weirdo. I would prefer to spend more time with my cows and my family and less time sitting on a tractor scraping manure.

One big upside in my world is when a few anti-dairy-farming types who have watched my videos start to understand the disconnect between what they had been fed by the activists and what is really going on here in Tillamook. Changing a mindset or an internal narrative takes a great deal of time and willpower. The new stories we tell ourselves need continuous support with repetition and exposure to the truth. A person's ability to remain anchored in denial is remarkable. Even when faced with reality, these stubborn people cling to their false narrative; they fiercely deem it as their own "truth."

I have had some interactions with people who are in the early stages of perspective change. They will write things to me like, "Well, okay...you might do things different, but you're not a factory farm."

I think their intention is to somehow bracket me off form the larger dairy operations, like the one at Fair Oaks Farm in Indiana, which milks roughly 30,000 cows each day. In their mind, it is the only way they can reconcile their hatred of dairy farming with their acceptance of what I have been telling them. They might even like me, which has to throw them into an unresolvable tailspin. They need to tell themselves that Wilsonview Farm is doing everything correctly, but that big, corporate, evil, FACTORY farms are still abusing their cows by confining them while they eat. They add to it all the other atrocities spouted by activists, too.

Despite that, the fact remains that I run my farm as a CAFO, just like most other dairy farms in the United States. I know for a fact that every single dairy farm in Oregon is a CAFO. Okay, there might be a small organic farm or two that tries to stick to a completely free-range setup with their cows, but take my word for it—our weather is not conducive to open sky feeding.

Before I go any further, let me hone in on an important point regarding CAFOs. Technically, I will officially become a CAFO once the infrastructure upgrade has been completed on the farm. For the time-being, the size of my farm is categorically an AFO (Intensive Animal Feeding Operation). To be even more specific, my 500 cows falls into the "medium-sized" AFO category.

For all the nerds that want to know the specifics of everything, here is the definition of AFO. This comes straight out of the Code of Federal Regulations, volume 68, number 1, page 7265:

- *Animals (other than aquatic animals) have been, are, or*
  will be stabled or confined and fed or maintained for a total of 45 days or more in any 12-month period, and
- *Crops, vegetation, forage growth, or post-harvest residues are not sustained in the normal growing season over any portion of the facility*
  (Agricultural Marketing Services, 2020).

To close the loop, here is the official definition of a CAFO:

...over 1,000 animal units are confined for over 45 days a year. An animal unit is the equivalent of 1,000 pounds of "live" animal weight.[1] A thousand animal units equates to 700 dairy cows, 1,000 meat cows, 2,500 pigs weighing more than 55 pounds (25 kg), 10,000 pigs weighing under 55 pounds, 10,000 sheep, 55,000 turkeys, 125,000 chickens, or 82,000 egg laying hens or pullets
(Natural Resources Conservation Service, n.d.).

Until the farm reaches 1,000 cows (which will probably happen by the time this book is published), I won't fall under the full definition of CAFO as set forth by the government.

This next part gets tricky. I am currently designated as a CAFO because of how my herd has the potential to affect the water system. This distinction is given by the Environmental Protection Agency (EPA) and the individual state where the farm is located. An AFO falls into the CAFO category when two conditions are met:

1. Pollutions are discharged into waters of the United States through a man-made flushing system, or other similar device.

2. Pollutants are discharged directly into waters of the United States which originate outside of and pass over, across, or through the facility or otherwise come into direct contact with the animals confined in the operation.

Our wastewater has the potential of coming into contact with surface water. As a result, I still follow all of the same rules and regulations like any official CAFO.

Sorry about all the technical gobbledygook, but it helps draw clear lines in the sand when it comes to permits, audits, and inspections. While I generally dislike the government looking over my shoulder, I do understand the importance of maintaining a clean water supply in our country.

For anyone who thinks the government can be lax in their approach to oversight, I want you to know that I get it. What makes this one better is that the State of Oregon has its own CAFO program. This means that our farm is regulated, visited, inspected, and audited by two governing bodies. We get the federal inspectors, and we also get state inspectors. Layers upon layers of government involvement, all watching to make sure we take care of our cows, take care of the soil, and take care of the water.

The next time you see one of the activist videos about how farmers appear to be fringe lunatics, think through the video critically. The activists want you to believe that farmers are free to indulge their mad pleasures against their innocent herd and destroy the land their herd lives on. They don't want you to know about the regulations and oversight.

Always remember: This is why we have the layers and layers of government.

The CAFO program is specifically about clean water. It is overseen by the United States Department of Agriculture (USDA). For all intents and purposes, it regulates how we dispose of our cow pee and poop.

So, how does waste disposal relate to feeding cows in a barn?

Good question!

Some beef cattle operations, and some worldwide dairy operations, let their cattle feed on the open range. They will mostly graze on prairie grasses and have their diets supplemented with baled hay, nutrient-rich feed, or other silage. When those cows poop and pee, their waste is left scattered around the prairie, and it disintegrates naturally into fertilizer over time.

In Oregon, our weather cannot support grazing year-round. So, we bring the cows indoors to feed them. As I mentioned earlier, we feed them less silage in the summer than in the winter precisely because they free-graze on their own when grasses are available. When winter hits, grasses become sparse, so we lay out more feed in the barn.

Either way, a cow's gotta eat.

Cows that eat in barns tend to poop and pee in barns. This creates wastewater which has to be disposed of in a manner that is a) consistent with the government regulations of CAFOs, but b) socially responsible, so as to not contaminate any of the drinking water that our community relies upon. We have to keep detailed records on how we store and distribute the waste. We have to maintain huge storage tanks, and then fertilize our fields using the waste in a careful and regulated manner.

After filing your yearly income taxes, you probably think the IRS loves details. The USDA and EPA make the IRS look as sloppy as Oscar

Madison. I have to keep track of when we apply the wastewater, what crops I grew, which of those crops received the wastewater fertilizer, what my soil samples indicate, and on, and on, ad nauseum.

Believe me when I say we are constantly testing, recording, and turning over records to one governmental agency or another. We have three large tanks earmarked specifically for wastewater, with a total combined capacity of 2.5 million gallons.

Let that wash over you for a minute. By the end of winter, we have accumulated 2.5 million gallons of raw cow sewage.

We farmers know how to party.

The tanks are completely empty at the beginning of winter, as per CAFO regulations. They get filled to capacity during the winter, and then completely emptied during the spring. Warm-weather months allow us to distribute the manure in a manner that allows for natural absorption and breakdown of the waste.

During the winter, our ground tends to be saturated from the rains; therefore, we are not allowed to spread manure because it cannot soak in or break down. The saturated ground means we cannot distribute the waste because it may run off into lakes and streams.

The conditions under which we are allowed to spread manure in the fields are very specific, and often under the watchful eyes of Uncle Sam. We don't have a government agent driving around behind our tractors, making sure we aren't disobeying the rules on any given day. Nor are any Men in Black hiding in the bushes with binoculars. But the local inspector lives here in town, and he does randomly drive-by every now and then to make sure we are operating within the guidelines.

CAFOs cannot be demonized by the activists for their impact on the water supply; that would imply that our wonderful government is somehow flawed and cannot enforce their own rules. So instead, the activists take a stand against what is, in my honest opinion, a strength of CAFOs.

Their complaint is that we are confining animals.

That's right. We have animals. In barns. Confined!

Once again, I wish we had a needle-scratch sound effect to play here. Or a "duh-duh-DUMMM!" byte of ominous music.

Their complaint boils down to the fact that the cows can wander indoors to eat. I realize that's not how cows used to eat—you know, before barns were invented. In my eyes, that's actually a good thing.

First of all, the cows are free to come and go as they please. We don't rope them, drag them into the barn, shackle them to the wall, and then laugh hysterically while we slam and bolt the doors behind them. Instead, the cows know where the food lives. When they feel like eating, they eat. When they feel like wandering off and doing whatever it is that cows do all day, they do that.

Second, the cows are perfectly equipped to handle all sorts of weather conditions. In fact, they are better equipped than humans to adapt to environmental change. In the winter, they will grow thick coats to protect them from the cold. Horses do the same thing, which is why you'll often see horses wearing blankets during winter months. The rancher doesn't want the aesthetic of a thick furry coat, so they keep their horse's body warm enough that their summer/fall coat will stay.

Likewise, cows can handle hot weather. Their bodies may change, but they adapt and move on. It's only when extreme conditions hit without warning that we have a problem, as evidenced by the snap of sweltering weather we had here recently.

Cows can live indoors or outdoors. I get it. However, it is more comfortable for them to lie around in the warm indoors when it's cold. They also prefer the shaded barn, complete with fans and an awesome cow brush, when it's hot outside.

I guess the activists hate comfortable cows.

One last important point I want to make is...(cover your ears) EVERY SINGLE HUMAN LIVES IN A CAFO. A city is a human CAFO. A town is a human CAFO. Heck, most arenas and theaters are human CAFOs. We all waltz merrily from one indoor facility to another. From the grocery store to church to school to home, we allow ourselves to be herded and passed through different facilities in our zip-coded CAFOs.

Why do we allow ourselves to be treated this way? Because it is a lot more comfortable to do things indoors. A picnic is nice once in awhile (okay, that's a lie—I hate them), but we don't picnic every day because the convenience of our kitchen table makes it a more desirable option.

In my mind, keeping the cows comfortable is more important than having them do what their ancestors did hundreds of years ago. Here again, we return to the notion of technological advancement. Farmers and their cows now have choices. We have machines that generate heat in the winter. We can build larger barns out of better materials, thereby creating more space for more cows to escape the cold if they choose to do so. We have large storage facilities and distribution chains so we can continue to feed our cows when the grass outdoors is buried under a foot of snow.

Our government has regulations in place to manage human waste just like they do with livestock waste. Because nature sometimes creates calamities and humans sometimes make errors (either accidentally or on purpose), raw human sewage will sometimes get released into the water systems.

The protocols aren't perfect; we abide by them on the farm unless something extreme happens. For example, if our valley floods and it affects our barns, we get the cattle to higher ground until the waters recede. In the meantime, the flood waters will carry out any cow waste that happens to be left behind scattered around the floor. We have no control over that act of God, and thereby are not "responsible" for a small amount of cow poop getting pushed raw into the water system. Outside of a disaster like that, we are diligent to collect, store, and distribute the waste within the guidelines set forth by the USDA and EPA.

The next time you hear the term CAFO used in a derogatory manner toward dairy farms, keep these ideas in mind. If you're the type of person who believes everything the activists say because you don't want to like dairy farms, then take in this information and chew on it for awhile before you spit it back out because it tastes bad.

I don't know why the lies tasted better in the first place.

But, that's just me.

Chapter 10
The Red Barn Complex

You ever wonder why barns are painted red? The answer may surprise you. Before you try to guess the answer, I will say it is not so the cows can find their way home. That response always amuses me. Cows are color blind.

Tell you what. I'm going to keep you in suspense for the time being. I tend to lose my train of thought rather easily, and I don't want to venture too far off the path before I complete my mental checklist.

Keep that red paint question in the back of your head. In the meantime, I'll tie together the concepts of red barns and sustainability.

***

I have one last point about sustainability that relates to a complete fabrication. This needs to be hit head-on. This myth was created and fostered by Madison Avenue and Hollywood. I call it "The Red Barn Complex" (RBC) because it seems common folks have been duped into thinking that farm life is nothing but a rural utopia; a glorious time capsule, affording a glimpse into bygone days of innocence, romance, and simple pleasures. A place where the skies are as clear and sunny as Mr. Farmer's friendly disposition. A place where…

oh no…

hang on…

Green Acres is the place to be!

Farm livin' is the life for me!

Land spreadin' out so far and wide!

Sorry about that. My life is so magical, I sometimes spontaneously break into song.

***

How does RBC manifest? Let's try a quick exercise.

Well…not all of you. Many people reading this book will be from farming backgrounds. I'll ask that group to kindly sit this one out. They have been faced with the reality of farm life and can see through all the RBC garbage. The rest of the readers might be from urban centers, suburbia, or other places where farming is less common. These are the folks I would like to try this exercise with me.

Wanna play along at home?

Okay! Name every farm cliché and Hollywood farming trope you can think of in the next thirty seconds. I'll write them down here. Ready…go!

Bibbed overalls

Straw hats

Stalk of wheat in the mouth

Smiling kids

Eating outdoors, at a long picnic-style table with a red-and-white checkered tablecloth

Lush green pastures

Smiling/talking animals

Pitchforks

Shining sun and gentle, cooling breeze

Pleasant, middle-aged farmer

Wife wears an apron; watches over happy, cooperative kids; cooks wholesome meals

Rope swings/tire swings

I'm sure there are many, many others. Anything from Norman Rockwell's body of work to every ad you see for "farm-fresh whatever" to television programs or pop culture paintings like American Gothic have colored our view of life on the farm.

In my language, this can all be summed up as "a life of sunshine and rainbows."

I understand the angle that advertisers take when they portray our life in a manner that suggests family values, happiness, and a salt-of-the-earth existence. They want to make famers seem relatable, and make their products seem like cogs in a wheel of tranquility and mental/physical/spiritual health for anyone who consumes them.

Will you chuckle at how cute and cuddly cows are? Maybe you'll buy more milk.

Will you watch a farmer tip his cap back and take a long satisfying drink of ice cold lemonade? Maybe you'll think of their frozen concentrate next time you're thirsty or passing their canisters in the supermarket.

Will you see a perfectly coiffed farm wife fluffing a tablecloth in the yard, preparing for another smile-filled family meal? Maybe you'll think about taking care of your family's financial future and purchase their life insurance.

Good vibes sell, and farmers are apparently surrounded by them all the time. Think about how many clichés are present when a lazy set designer wants to create a set to shoot a farm scene. They call up the props department, order a few hay bales and horseshoes, and then prepare to assemble the cast for a good ol' fashioned hoedown!

Or a barn-raisin'.

Or the miraculous birth of an adorable tiny pink piglet.

136

Or whatever.

I'm getting a headache just writing these words. Although honestly, newborn piglets are kind of cute.

You might be reading this and waiting for me to get to the point. After all, what could be so bad about people thinking that farmers lead an idyllic life? Americans value the qualities of hard work and family unity, so those are good characteristics to attribute to me and my brothers-in-farms.

Generally speaking, farmers do tend to be friendly and helpful. So why harsh everyone's buzz?

Great question! Here's why: people are duped into believing that farm life is akin to Disneyland. Clean, welcoming, pure. So, when they have to somehow reconcile that notion with an image of a dead cow or of a difficult calving, they cannot bear the thought of their nirvana being tainted.

The friction of those mental tectonic plates grinding against each other is what spews out an emotional discharge that gets blown up on social media. When a person's expectation of a dancing cow singing along with Gene Kelly runs into a video of a farmer performing artificial insemination, the person is aghast.

Honestly, anyone is going to be uncomfortable with some of the things I see and do every day or every week. I certainly am. But people who understand that life has both triumph and tragedy will be able to make their peace with the uglier parts of our existence. And the uglier parts of farming.

Do you feel grief-stricken when (knock on wood) your mother passes away? I'm sure you do. Can you handle it and move on with your life? Again, it'll be tough, but I'm sure you can.

Why? Losing a parent is certainly a great tragedy in our life cycle. Why do so many people lose a mother and not lose their mind? Why do they not demand a change in the laws governing life and death? Why do they not issue death threats on social media to the doctors and nurses and administrators who looked after their ill mother? Why do they not dedicate their lives to posting YouTube videos of aides spoon-feeding Alzheimer's patients or of cancer patients vomiting after chemotherapy treatments or of bodies on gurneys and sporting toe tags in a morgue?

The answer: we expect to outlive our parents. We don't like it. We try to deny it. Of course, my parents are going to live forever. But when it happens, it isn't like we had no way to prepare ourselves for this eventuality, or that we had no idea this could ever happen, or that a "just God" would never allow this sort of atrocity to occur.

No. We get it. We hate it, but we get it. Our reality matches our expectation.

I will bet every single one of your parents will agree with me. Losing a parent is tough, but it 100% absolutely beats the alternative. Parents do not want to outlive their children. I cannot imagine a more painful event to try to get over. That is not in accordance with our expectations. Children outlive their parents.

End of story.

Do you want to know my reality?

I've already detailed several unpleasant parts of my reality. From dead cows to stillborn calves, to going elbow-deep into a cow's anus, there is a lot to endure when you're a farmer. But let's not overlook the more subtle aspects of my day.

Let's begin with the smell. Have you ever been to a farm? Many of you haven't, and that's fine. Have you ever been to the livestock area at a county or state fair? Probably quite a few more of you have done that.

The first thing you notice is a smell that is symptomatic of livestock. And, also ubiquitous in and around the barn. The smell isn't overpowering, but it lingers like a fetid blanket over the entire operation. It's a combination of musky cow, moist waste (poop and pee), and hay.

It never goes away. But you get used to it.

The second thing you notice on the farm is all the bugs. They never seem to make mention of the flying nuisance machines on television or in magazine ads. Livestock attract bugs, especially flying bugs. They are swarming around the barn and the fields, picking through manure and trying to poke their way into my eyes and ears. There isn't much we can do about the problem, short of napalming the entire property every few months.

That just seems cost-prohibitive. Have you priced napalm recently?

That was joke, people.

Fortunately, I live in a climate that isn't as conducive to bugs as the Midwest. I can't imagine the Biblical plague conditions those farmers have to work in.

The third thing you notice is that everyone on the farm is tired and often grumpy toward one another. Brusque, at the very least. I'm probably exaggerating a little here because I'm writing this segment before my coffee has had a chance to fully soak in. But we're talking about people who get up several hours before dawn, and then proceed to work a ten- or twelve-hour day, seven days a week. And I mean every day. Thanksgiving and Christmas included.

To be fully transparent, it's relentless. We never (well, rarely) think about how relentless it can be. If we dwelled upon that thought, we would grow pretty depressed. Instead, we just keep getting up and keep going to work. Seriously, farming is more of a lifestyle than an occupation. For us, farming is life.

Last of all: stuff breaks. I know the television shows and magazine ads show shiny painted tractors, sealed barns, and equipment that comes to life every time you push the button. In my world, there seems to always be something breaking. The tractor squeals when you push the brake pedal, or the barn needs repair, or the irrigation system springs a leak. My day would run so much more smoothly if everything worked every time I turned it on. I don't see my wife and kids nearly enough as it is. It irritates me to take more time away from them because Dad and I end up doing stupid maintenance or repair work. Those jobs don't get factored into our work day; they are added to our work day.

Fortunately, we are making enough profit these days (there's that word again) that we can assign certain tasks to employees, or outsource to someone in town. When our septic tank bit the big one, we hired an excavation company to dig out the old one and install the new one. That option is a luxury. I never take it for granted.

Don't get me wrong. I'm not complaining. I love what I do and would lose my mind if I had to sell insurance or sit behind a computer all day or drive a school bus filled with 35 or 40 screaming kids every morning. I respect the people who do all of those jobs. But farm livin' is the life for me.

Don't worry. I won't sing again. For now, anyway.

Next time you come face-to-face with an activist video that manipulates the sentimentality of people who nurture this false image of our perfect farm life, shake your head. Watch with a perspective based in reality. Most farmers are doing their very best to keep the herd happy and healthy, but sometimes bad things happen to good cows.

Just like people.

***

The notion of "the perfect farm" is an idealistic delusion shared by many who have never set foot on a farm. Activists know this, thus they use shock tactics to shatter the delusion. When the idyllic delusion is ripped from the viewer, it opens the door for those activists with ulterior motives. These opportunists exploit the viewer's emotional distress to peddle their perspective.

As you can surmise, that perspective is not based in reality.

Buzzwords like "regenerative," "grass-fed," and "organic" are conjured up, then foisted upon the public—even by advertising agencies. The message under the buzzword is that farms such as mine are "bad," and farms (such as the ones supporting their product) are "good."

Some of you may be old enough to remember Certs, a hard candy that doubled as a breath mint. The commercials proclaimed that Certs was the superior mint because it contained Retsyn ("Certs has Retsyn!"). It was a fairly big ad campaign back in the 1960s and 1970s. The candy company's marketing department wanted to somehow separate Certs from the other candy/breath mint options at the checkout counter. Almost overnight, Retsyn became a household word. Everyone knew the phrase, "Certs has Retsyn!" It became a good reason to purchase Certs instead of Tic Tacs or spearmint flavored chewing gum. The impression given by the advertisement was that Retsyn was some kind of exotic, orally hygienic super-chemical, and that you totally wanted it!

However, I don't remember anyone ever asking the question, "What the heck is Retsyn, anyway? And is it something I want in the first place?"

Most people would be surprised to find out that Retsyn is a mixture of copper gluconate, partially hydrogenated cottonseed oil, and flavoring. In fact, it was the copper gluconate that created the green flecks on the otherwise white candy (Warner Lambert Co. vs United States, 2005).

Retsyn was a trademarked name created by the manufacturer of Certs to label one of their proprietary ingredients. The word sounded proper, official, and a little mysterious, so they used it to market their product.

In a supreme twist of irony, Retsyn was partially responsible for the demise of Certs. The candy was discontinued in 2018, when partially hydrogenated cottonseed oil was no longer allowed as a food ingredient in the United States (FDA Final Determination, 2015).

That's not the only famous example of deceptive marketing. Dodge has a big campaign around their "Hemi" engines. Anyone know what a Hemi is? No? Anyone ever pair that word with big, throaty, manly workhorse trucks? Sure. That makes it an effective campaign.

Incidentally, the word Hemi refers to engines with hemispheric combustion chambers and domed cylinder heads. This configuration gives more power at high RPMs, but loses efficiency at normal RPMs. It will get you from zero-to-sixty under load (like when you're towing something big or have the bed filled with heavy materials) because the engine is more efficient when stress is applied. But it is less efficient when you are just rolling along with the cruise control set at 65. Thus, the Hemi engine has its pros and cons. But why get lost in the details of reality when you can boast "I have a Hemi!" to your friends and relatives?

It might also surprise you to know that the Hemi design has been around since the 1950s, and that several manufacturers (not just Chrysler) have produced cars which have that same engine design. Dodge trucks don't have the market cornered; they were just the first ones to create an ad campaign around that particular buzzword.

All throughout the history of advertising, a variety of gimmicks have been used to give a product a unique identity. Slogans ("Melts in your mouth, not in your hands"), characters ("Let's ask Mr. Owl!"), celebrities (Shaquille O'Neal for everything from Icy Hot to Taco Bell), jingles ("My bologna has a first name..."), and humor (the Budweiser "Whassup" ad) are all employed to make a product stand out. It's what advertising agencies do, and they're good at it.

Our industry is no different ("Got Milk?"). Dairy farmers want to sell dairy products; cattle farmers want to sell beef; large farms everywhere want to sell fruits, vegetables, and other animal products. So when smaller farms pop up all over the countryside, they also need to stand out.

Of course, they should have the chance to earn a living. I just wish they wouldn't implicitly trash the bigger farmers to do so. Often, this process involves creating a buzzword that elicits an emotional reaction, and then pits the little guy (good guy) against the bigger guy (bad guy). It becomes the usual trope of David versus Goliath.

Consumers who may not know any better are convinced to pay a premium for products produced by smaller farms. However, those small-farm products, for all intents and purposes, are the same as the ones produced by larger farms. Again, I'm not trying to belittle anyone making a buck or two. Rather, I am trying to shine a light on a truth so that consumers can make an informed decision instead of falling for deceptive advertising techniques.

I really want to stress that I am not trying to put these other farmers out of business—I would never do that. I have mentioned that I do not judge how another person chooses to live their life, as long as it doesn't encroach upon mine. What I dislike is all the bare-faced lying that goes on with farming, and the use of meaningless, empty corporate buzzwords.

Regenerative

This is the newest of the focus-group supported corporate buzzwords. Like the word "sustainable," I don't think this word has a consistent, concrete meaning. Its vague definition makes it the perfect marketing tool; it forces the consumer to draw their own conclusions about the meaning. It creates an emotional reaction instead of educating the consumer. The implication of the word is more important than the word itself.

That implication opens the door for smaller farms to market themselves against us. I'm not punching down at the little guy, but a ten-acre farm that tries to hype how much more regenerative they are than the bigger farms is either misinformed or lying. They have less land to care for and fewer animals to manage less waste, but they aren't practicing any ideals that we don't adhere to every day.

There is not—nay, there cannot—be a farm that has been in a family for four, six, or ten generations that is not regenerative. That simply couldn't happen. All of the legacy farms are, by definition, regenerative. We have to take care of the soil. We have to take care of the livestock. We have to take care of the water. There is no way to survive as a farm if we scorch the earth behind us.

If advertisers want to frame our farming practices as not regenerative (and by contrast, frame their clients' farms as models of regenerativity), then they are just plain wrong. They are not lying to you outright; they are lying through sleight of hand. These are lies of omission, which are just as intentional.

Ask anyone who has ever been cheated on by a spouse. Plenty of important details are purposefully obscured during a conversation. When you ask what they did that day, they don't say they didn't meet their lover for a lunchtime quickie. That would be an outright lie. So instead, they just don't talk about lunch.

Not an overt lie. Just a convenient omission.

The truth is, the smaller farms can be perfectly regenerative. I don't have any reason to believe that the gentleman farmer is not taking care of the soil, water, or animals. In fact, my default thought process would be in the exact opposite direction. I would think small farmers are ethical farmers until I am proven otherwise.

I just wish they would give me the same consideration. The current political winds make it so we are guilty until—and even after—we are proven innocent. The court of public opinion is skewed, and some people don't care to know the truth. They know their truth, and punish us for their distorted reality.

One activist can fabricate one video of a farmer "destroying" the water table. I can then produce and show 100 videos that provide proof that the activist video is complete crap. But those who live by "their" truth don't want evidence. They don't want proof. They don't want to be shown they are incorrect.

They only want justice. At any cost.

Grass-Fed

Here is another one that makes me chuckle. Beef and dairy products will have another 20% or so tagged onto their prices if they are advertised as "grass-fed." Consumers eat that stuff up, even though the notion itself is silly to me. Somehow, people have been convinced that cows fed only grass are somehow superior to cows that are fed a mixture of grass and grain.

A lot of confusion is purposefully created to befuddle the consumer between buzzwords like "grass-fed", "free-range" and "pasture-raised." When these farmers want to justify another price hike, they'll ask the marketing agency to invent another word to use that will convince the consumer to part ways with a few more dollars.

However, I will admit that grass-fed beef does have a different flavor. In this instance, the advertising campaign has a valid point. There is a difference. However, that difference creates an interesting conundrum for the consumer.

To my tongue, grain-fed tastes better than grass fed. Beef from grain-fed cows has a more flavorful fat, thereby making the meat more succulent to the palate. Grass-fed cows are going to be leaner in general. The meat won't be marbled with delicious fats like grain-fed will be.

Both types of beef are nutritionally similar. Notice I said "similar" and not "identical." Grass-fed beef does have a slight edge when it comes to certain ingredients, but that edge is smaller than you may have been led to believe.

For example, grass-fed beef is sometimes touted for having higher levels of Omega-3 fatty acids than grain-fed beef.

This statement is true.

How much of a difference? Grass-fed beef contains about 65mg of Omega-3s. Grain-fed beef has about 35mg. At face value, you'd think, "Holy cow! Grass-fed beef has double the amount of Omega-3s!" (Roach, 2021).

You would be correct. But, let's ask another relevant question: Is that amount going to make a real difference in your diet?

No USRDA standard has been set, but the Institute of Medicine recommends that adult men get 1,600mg of Omega-3 fatty acids per day in their diet. Just for the sake of comparison, a single serving of salmon contains 1,800-2,000mg of Omega-3s (Roach, 2021).

So is a difference of 30mg going to make a difference in my diet? Mathematically, yes.

Is it going to make huge impact? Arguably, no.

There actually is a noticeable taste difference in the beef produced by grass-fed cows. It's ironic to me, but consumers are willing to pay a premium for that difference, despite the difference being a negative rather than a positive. Paying more for less tasty meat sounds like a loss rather than a win.

But again, that's just me.

Organic

This is a topic I have touched upon, but it is worth revisiting here. An organic farmer is one that does not use chemical fertilizers in the soil, pesticides on their crops, or antibiotics and/or hormones in their livestock. The philosophy goes back to the origins of farming when these products were not commercially available, mainly because they hadn't been invented yet.

In my mind, the undertaking of the organic farmer is a noble one. They have to work hard to raise their products the old-fashioned way. Farms were small back then, exactly because the work was so hard.

I speak for myself and my farm only when I say that we do not engage in organic farming. We like to have other tools in our toolbox. We like to have options for when things don't go exactly as planned. We like to give medicine to sick cows so they'll feel better.

I must strongly stress that farms do not preemptively feed antibiotics to their livestock. They aren't allowed to do that, even if they wanted to. For dairy farmers specifically, the USDA tests every tanker of milk. Plus, every animal is tested for antibiotics before it or its milk goes to consumers.

Chicken farms and pig farms are run the exact same way. With government oversight being so tight, the bio-security at some of the larger grow operations is insane. Large operation livestock farmers cannot risk an infection to their animals. Quarters are tight and any infectious disease would spread like wildfire. One or two sick chickens would immediately require that 20,000 need to be treated for the infection. That is cost prohibitive, so management takes extreme measure to ensure that no pathogens are ever introduced to the livestock.

I know first-hand that some of the bigger pig farms in the Midwest require all workers to go through a dress-down and clean up room before entering the livestock area. They put on new clothes, which are decontaminated daily, once they enter the facility.

If sickness gets introduced to a single animal, it would depopulate an entire barn. That's a lot of animals and money flying out of the farmer's pocket.

Also, organic farms do not using synthetic chemicals on their crops.

From my perspective, it's very beneficial to control pests or give the soil a little boost by using synthetic chemicals.

Don't be fooled into thinking that organic farms do not use chemicals. They do. They use naturally-sourced chemicals rather than man-made synthetic chemicals. However, no farmer can rely on crops that are devoid of any pesticides. Their fruits or vegetables would get gobbled up by bugs and worms if there weren't a chemical barrier to protect them.

Given the technological and chemical advances made over the past twenty or thirty years, synthetic chemicals have become more effective and less environmentally destructive than their predecessors. Our desire to take care of the soil and the water has led farmers to seek out better, more efficient synthetics to help raise good products while reducing environmental impact.

Organic farming is indeed different, and honestly, it can be better in some respects than larger farming operations. However, the difference may not be as intense as you'd think.

Make your own choices. I am a big fan of some things the smaller farmers are doing. I like the notion of farming the way our ancestors did. It's a good throwback to the purity of the industry. Larger farms don't do things in a bad way. Organic farmers have a seat at the table.

I just don't like when the truth gets bent.

***

Have you been mulling over the reason barns are painted red? Just like the myth of RBC, the answer is far less "charmed" than you'd think.

The real reason is pragmatic rather than romantic. The real reason is money. The red paint cost less than white paint. Back in the day, white paint was colored using white lead, which was pricey. The red paint got its color from—wait for it—rust (Baker, n.d.).

I'm not even kidding.

Farmers would mix a little linseed oil with the rust-tinged paint, and their wood barns would be fortified against decay. Not a perfect science, but clever nonetheless. In fact, the actual red paint was more of a burnt reddish/orange hue than the fire-engine red color we think of today (Baker, n.d.).

Barns were big, so very costly to paint. In fact, many farmers opted to not paint their barns for this very reason. Not all barns were red (Baker, n.d.).

However, the linseed oil was necessary to help preserve the wood and it needed to be diluted into a base. Many farmers would reluctantly spend some money on paint. Red was the cheapest, and there you go (Baker, n.d.).

As an aside, farmhouses are almost universally painted white. White paint was more expensive, but there is still a bit of pragmatism sprinkled in.

First, farmers still needed to coat the wood with linseed oil. Therefore, they needed a paint base to dilute the linseed oil into and spread it. Also, the farm house was much smaller than the barn, so they splurged on a paint color that created an image of cleanliness. The lead and zinc-oxide that tinted the white paint made it last longer than any other color. It was also easier to touch up.

I've been in farming for my entire life, but I have never owned, nor have I ever seen, a red barn. If you've ever driven across the Midwest, you have probably seen dozens of dilapidated barns getting reclaimed by the earth. Sagging giants, they wither away, forgotten and left behind against a backdrop of technology and societal change.

But, none of them are red. Most are various shades of darkening grey, blackened by the relentless march of time and corrosive effects of weather. If any red paint had been used back then, it has worn away.

Many barns were not red in the first place. Somewhere along the way, the quaint image of a red barn with white trim has been burned into our collective psyche. The paint is flawless, and the wood is perky and well-fitting.

I don't think barns ever looked like the ones seen in advertising. They weren't that perfect when they were first built, much less so after a year or two of four-season meteorological abuse.

Hey, I'm no monster. Enjoy your singing cows and cartoon farm family wonderlands. Like everything else I am touting in this book, all I ask is for everyone to be a rational and curious consumer of information. Please, don't be that person who swallows everything they see and hear without so much as chewing. I don't know why there are some people who would be shocked to learn that not everything they see on the internet is true. Or that only the things they disagree with are lies. Given that you are reading this book, I would guess you're not one of those.

Now, if you'll excuse me, I have to go lean on a perfect split-rail fence and talk to my lantern-jawed neighbor who always seems to have a five-o'clock shadow, even right after he shaves. We'll both be wearing crisp, freshly laundered flannel shirts and key bib overalls, which are stain-free with a razor-sharp crease down the front and back. We'll spit tobacco juice while we mop our foreheads with the brightly colored bandanas conveniently tied around our necks. We'll laugh and laugh and slap each other on the back while we chat. Probably about another hysterical caper as hijinks ensue on our respective farms.

Chapter 11
Carbon Credits

Welcome to the most complex economic and environmental issue covered in this book: carbon credits. The Merriam-Webster Dictionary defines carbon credit as a tradable credit granted to a holder to incentivize reducing emissions of greenhouse gases (n.d.).

In very simple terms, a carbon credit is a permit or a certification that allows a company or a country to emit one ton of greenhouse gas. If the company goes over an established limit of emissions, they can trade credits with another company that hasn't reached the limit.

The United States has no federal requirements for using carbon credits (but, give it time; that could change). All the government does is establish the limit of the emission. It's up to the holder of the carbon credits to decide how to take care of the emissions. Participation in any carbon credit program is voluntary (Conniff, 2009).

The history of the carbon credit is just as convoluted as its definition. It came from an early 20th century idea of making industry pay for the damage that their pollution caused during the Industrial Revolution. In the 1960s, economist John Dales evolved the idea further by using tradable permits to motivate the industries to clean up. The problem of acid rain arose in the late 1980s, thus reviving the "cap-and-trade" idea. The process was streamlined to allow the trading of the permit credits to be done in a "free-market" manner. The Clean Air Act of 1990, drafted by a conservative multimillionaire and an environmentalist, made this form of emissions trading legal in the United States. Since then, the trading of carbon credits to control emissions of greenhouse gases has been implemented in the same manner worldwide, all while avoiding government regulations (Conniff, 2009).

I don't have a problem with the concept of carbon credits. I am not opposed to this philosophy at all. I am a farmer, after all, so taking care of the earth is directly in line with how I make my living. Taking pollution out of the atmosphere is a very good thing, and I appreciate everyone who does their part to keep our world clean. Many companies create sound infrastructures to reduce their emissions. At the behest of the government (politicians also listen to the wishes of their constituents), several technological advances have been made with recycling, filtering, eliminating, and refining operations to become more environmentally friendly.

However, what I do have a problem with is the rampant deception and bald-faced hypocrisy that takes place surrounding carbon credits.

For a start, carbon credits are not an equal, one-to-one exchange when it comes to emissions versus climate change. A common way for companies to offset their emissions is to pay to have a forest planted in another country, the idea being that the trees will absorb the carbon dioxide emitted. But, carbon dioxide isn't the only greenhouse gas emitted by these companies. The other gases emitted are methane, nitrous oxide, ozone, and fluorocarbons (Sovacool, 2011).

This leads to the next problem. Notice that the company trading credits makes no mention of anything they are doing in their own process to reduce the carbon emissions they produce. Instead, they pay a second company to do the work of reducing the overall worldwide carbon footprint.

When a company announces that their greenhouse gas production (or whatever pollutant they produce) has been reduced by a certain percent, they'll put out a press release. Carefully read the way the way one of these press releases is worded; they don't state directly that they have slashed the emissions coming from their own factory or office complex. It may read like this:

Because of our efforts to leave the planet in the same—or better—shape than we found it, the Widget Corporation was challenged to reduce our carbon footprint to zero by the year 2040. At that time, we will be absolutely carbon neutral. I'm happy to announce that today, we are well ahead of our projected pace! In fact, 2020 alone saw an overall reduction of 15% of greenhouse gas emissions, thanks to the efforts and sheer determination of all the dedicated employees at our Widget campus, and at our Widget manufacturing facility!

Interesting, right? The Widget Corporation spokesperson isn't lying. Technically, the Widget Corporation itself isn't actually doing a bad thing—they're doing a good thing. However, they are also bending the truth in how they present their information. It's just your everyday, garden-variety lie by omission.

What ends up being even more interesting is how these companies game the system. In my example here, the numbers are kept to round amounts for the sake of simplicity.

Let's say the Widget Corporation produces 1,000 metric tons of carbon emissions in any given year. They set a goal of reducing their carbon output to zero in ten years. This would mean changing something to reduce emissions by 100 metric tons per year (1,000 tons/10 years = 100 per year).

Another company, Acme, Inc., is investing in infrastructure to reduce their carbon footprint. Acme might need advanced equipment, develop new technology, change a manufacturing plant, or invest in new chemicals to change the way their waste products are broken down. Of course, emission reduction costs money. Acme, Inc. finds they must invest 1,000 dollars to reduce their carbon emissions by 25 metric tons per year.

What the Widget Corporation will do is find four companies just like Acme and pay each of them three thousand dollars so that they can take credit for each of the respective 25 tons of eliminated carbon. Bundled together, this means the Widget Corporation can take credit, as well as meet their goal, for an overall 100 ton reduction in carbon emissions per year.

And let's not forget that the Acme company (and the three others just like it) made three times the amount of money they needed to build their infrastructure.

Why would they do it this way? There're two reasons.

First, the Widget Corporation is massive. The infrastructure required to actually reduce their carbon footprint would run into millions of dollars. It would be cheaper to pay someone else to change their own infrastructure than doing it to their own.

Second, this is great press. Molding an ad campaign around the fact that the Widget Corporation is responsible for eliminating 100 tons of greenhouse gas emissions is a powerful selling point for their widgets. It makes people feel good to buy those widgets. And good vibes are more important than actual information when the general public makes decisions.

Third, this process makes the company look good to the government. The government of the country they're located in wants to reduce greenhouse gas emissions, too. The government, like the corporation, is heavily invested in public opinion. At the behest of their constituents, they implore corporations to reduce their carbon footprint.

The truth is, the government only cares that 100 tons of carbon has been taken out of the atmosphere. Once that's accomplished, the company and the government can tell the public that they are working in conjunction to make the world a better place! All without any need to get lost in the messy details of where those savings come from.

Let's not forget Acme and the other small companies that are paid to do the actual work. They turn a profit with the money they receive from the big corporations for doing what they were already going to do anyway. Even though their infrastructure changes only cost $1,000, they made $2,000 on top of it.

We have a win/win/win!

Unfortunately, there is one loser. That loser is you.

Yes, less carbon getting tossed haphazardly into the atmosphere. However, this comes at a cost, and you are the one to shoulder that burden.   Remember, companies are not in business to lose money. They exist to make money. If they are faced with an additional expense, such as tax increases, wage increases, or equipment upgrades, they raise the price of their product to cover the cost.

But, to add even more to your loser burden, this program can end up costing you, the consumer, even more than it should!

Let's take another look at Acme. We'll now call it a dairy farm. The Acme farmer needs to purchase a new truck. He knows that any truck has a shelf life. If he purchases a Chevy or Ford, it won't last forever. So, he sets aside a little money each quarter to build a "truck fund," so that when old Bessie dies, there's enough in his piggy bank to get another truck.

There's no sudden, upfront expense for the purchase of the truck. The cost has already been factored into his budget, which means it is already factored into the pricing structure of his product. Therefore, the new truck costs his consumer nothing additional.

The farmer decides to purchase one of the soon-to-be-available electric trucks instead of a diesel truck. His overall carbon footprint is now reduced because the electric truck produces zero emissions.

Yes, I know that manufacturing the truck, producing batteries, and using electricity requires plenty of energy that, in turn, creates plenty of emissions. But, please, let's not get lost in those weeds, either.

The Widget Corporation still offers to pay the farmer $3,000 for his carbon emission "savings." To the farmer, this is a windfall. He was going to buy a truck anyway, and now he's getting paid to do it? Heck yeah! Technically, his overall reduction in carbon emissions didn't create any additional cost. He was prepared to buy a new truck anyway, and he did.

However, the Widget Corporation is paying $3,000 for carbon credits that are already built into the financial/pricing structure of the farm. Thus, Widget is unnecessarily paying for something that isn't costing anyone anything. Widget is paying solely for the right to boast rather than paying to reduce any real carbon emission.

As a matter of fact, all costs involving credit carbons are passed on to the consumer. The government also gets their pound of flesh, as well. They tax the sale of carbon credits. Wall Street is also cut into this deal. Hedge funds broker the carbon credit deals, thereby making money on each transaction.

Who pays for the taxes and brokerage fees? Do I even need to say it again?

(Psst…you do).

Many companies in the carbon credit program have set a date for when their company will be "completely green" or "carbon neutral." Usually, that date is a decade or two in the future. But, can these companies really be completely carbon neutral by that time?

No. They can't. No office building, factory, or work from home business is totally carbon neutral to begin with. It is also impossible to completely eliminate a carbon footprint on a human timescale. Remember, one ton of carbon dioxide will remain in the atmosphere for about one thousand years on average (Sovacool, 2011).

If this is simply the way this system works, why does it irritate me so much?

I get irritated because farmers are not getting any credit for things we have been doing all along. Nobody understands that farming is among the most sustainable and regenerative industries in the world, and it always has been. Farmers are doing yeoman's work to actually save the planet. Farmers use no-till soil practices, install high efficiency lighting in the barn, or any number of other carbon-saving efforts that have developed over the past 10 to 15 years. Yet, we are cast as the villains who abuse the animals and the soil, and who pollute the water and the citizens.

I don't need to be praised for the work I do. You purchase my milk, and that works for me. I don't require applause,f ancy ceremonies, or press conferences on the steps of the Wilsonview Corporate headquarters to prove I'm all that and a bag of chips. I'm just not that insecure.

It drives me insane when corporations pay top dollar to cast themselves as "the heroes and the saviors of the planet" when they are actually doing nothing to honestly save the planet—except pay other people to do what they should be doing themselves.

Good lord, people; I wish everyone would wake up!

Write a big enough check, and the world forgives hypocrisy.

That's just my opinion. I really hope I'm wrong.

Chapter 12
A Day in the Life of a Cow

I hate to burst the bubble for anyone who's formed their understanding of cow behavior from watching cartoons and movies. They probably think cows spend a lot of time singing, dancing, playing catch with footballs or Frisbees, or wandering the countryside solving crimes. And for those people, thinking about cows that way makes them happy.

I like happy people, but I also like well-informed people.

Cows actually spend most of their time doing what many of you would do if all of your needs were constantly met. They lie around, relaxing and chewing their cud.

Okay. You might not chew cud. But substitute "Cheetos" for cud, and you'll immediately relate to the scenario.

Despite the cows' relative lack of abject excitement (or crime fighting ability), I'll walk you through a day in the life of a cow. I'll use mostly my own naturally keen powers of observation and deduction to lay out the facts, but there is a nice column by Erin Brown, Communications Director for the American Dairy Association Mideast, that will back up everything I say (Brown, n.d.). For all of you data freaks, she pulls actual scientific studies to support her points (Lee, 2011).

***

The start of a cow's day is a bit ambiguous because their sleep cycle molds itself around their daily routine. They know they'll get milked and fed twice per day, at the same times every day, so their lifestyle revolves around those two important items on their schedule.

Yes, cows do sleep. All organisms require time to unplug the switchboard and power down for a spell. However, probably like your pet dog at home, cows spend large chunks of their day resting and relaxing. Somewhere in the neighborhood of 14 hours per day is spend doing whatever the cow feels like doing, which is usually dozing lightly while they chew their cud.

If you watch my videos on Facebook, I emphasize that cows do actually sleep, despite the time of night or day I am filming. Even at 3:00am, the cows are up, wide-eyed and bushy-tailed. That may create the illusion that cows never sleep, but there's more to it than that.

They are also programmed to be up and running when they know it's time to be milked and fed. Like a tall, husky dinner chime, my presence alerts the cows, and they'll hurry to the buffet table.

Also, the cows graze based upon seasonal weather patterns. For example, when it's summertime, they will go out and graze at night when it's cooler. They will adjust to that by sleeping more during daylight hours.

During winter months, there isn't much to graze on. So cows will spend most of their day indoors where it's warm and dry. As a result, they'll sleep more when it's dark.

So yes, cows sleep just like you and I. They actually do us one better. Cows can be completely at rest while they stand. They are maybe not "asleep" per se, but they are totally powered down nonetheless.

This natural tendency of cows has given rise to one of the biggest shams in the history of farmers who interact with city clickers.

***

Has everyone heard of cow-tipping?

Of course you have.

Cows can "sleep" standing up, so rambunctious teenagers will run across a pasture and tip them over. The tipping process can be accomplished by either gently shoving the cow until she falls, or it could be more aggressive, leading to a shoulder-to-cow collision that will send the cow sprawling across the field until she lands on her side.

All great fun, right? Probably leads to teenagers howling with laughter.

In all truth, that last part is the only part that really happens.

The concept of "cow tipping" was dreamt up by bored farmers who were sitting around one day, wondering how to get city folks to do dumb things. And end up covered in cow poop.

So, they invented the urban myth of cow-tipping. And c'mon people—let's think this through.

An average teenage boy weighs around 160 pounds (~72kg). A Holstein weighs 1,500 pounds (~680 kg). I'm no physicist, but it seems like a collision of any magnitude between those two objects is not going to end well for the teenager.

To get an idea of what could happen, have your 160 pound teenager get down on all fours. If we keep the ratios the same, cow tipping would be like having a 17-pound (7.7 kg) dog try to knock him or her off their pins and onto the floor.

Now, let's say the 17-pound dog takes a running head start and slams into the teenager's shoulder. The force will no doubt stagger the teen, but who is going to be on the worse end of that dispersion of kinetic energy?

No farmer wants anyone to get hurt, especially their cows. Nor do they relish the idea of malicious teenagers running around on their property. However, the farmer will get the last laugh, as will the friends of whoever is tapped to try the cow tip. There aren't many other possible outcomes.

First of all, the tipper is going to have to make their way across a live pasture to get to the cow. In a perfect world, the cow would be dozing right next to the fence line, but this is rarely ever the case. Because cow tipping is always best done at night, the teen will be moving over the land in the dark.

Cow pastures are notorious for having piles of cow poop.

I know, right? That blows my mind.

The odds of the teen making it all the way across the pasture without ever stepping, slipping, or falling into a savory pile of cow poop is almost zero. They are going sustain some damage before even getting to the cow.

If the manure they hit while running is still wet, it will act as steamy brown ice (even in summer), sending the teen tumbling to the ground, and possibly into an adjacent pile of cow poop.

At this point, their friends are laughing hysterically.

But the teen might pick themselves up, squeegee as much poop form their clothes as possible, and continue toward the cow.

Let's say they make it to the cow. First of all, the cows might be dozing, but they are not dead. They are prey animals by nature, so their brain is constantly on alert for potential predators in the environment. A teenager, chugging across a pasture, possibly screaming in outrage when they land in a fresh pile of turds, will awaken the cows.

An awake cow isn't going to let a stranger near them without some sort of evasive maneuver. The cows will shift, walk, or move out of harm's way, thereby forcing the teen to travel a greater distance at a greater speed, thereby creating greater opportunity to discover new and undisturbed piles of cow manure.

By now, their friends have almost passed out because they are laughing so hard.

Let's say the teen does arrive cow-side. Do you really think a cow is going to stand there and let a pipsqueak tip it over?

No. Don't. Think. So.

Now, the teen will be chasing a cow around. If the teen manages to catch up, he'll lean into her, trying to get her off her feet. His feet will be sliding around, trying to find enough purchase to gain leverage. But that amount of leverage cannot be generated by a 160-pound foe.

In the end, they will most likely land on their wallet one final time, leading their friends to start convulsing with uncontrolled (and possibly deadly) laughter.

Do not overlook the fact that the teenager, in the throes of disappointment, still has to make it back across the pasture to exit the same way he entered. More darkness, more poop, and more opportunity for his friends to go viral with the resulting YouTube videos.

Trust me when I say this: first, cow-tipping isn't really a thing. Second, I have done this so many times to dumb friends of mine. It never disappoints.

And finally, yeah—a couple of beers may have been involved.

***

As I mentioned, cows spend a lot of time relaxing. Many animals do this, particularly after eating. Cows eat a lot, so they require a lot of down time to give their body an opportunity to process all the food.

You know how you feel after a big meal? You're probably a little sleepy. Think back to a Thanksgiving when you really over-indulged at the table. For me, this means most of them. After dinner, you waddle to a recliner, turn on either the Dallas or Detroit football game on network television, and pass out cold. Don't blame the tryptophan in the turkey. Digestion in general requires a lot of energy. When you pack your gut full of complex carbohydrates, your brain allocates all of your energy resources toward digestion. Other functions, like consciousness, take a back seat. Hence, you nap while your gut breaks down all the food.

How does this apply to cattle? Well, cows eat a lot of complex fibers (like cellulose) because their diet consists mainly of grasses, grains, and other complex plant materials. It takes a lot of time and energy to break those fibers down to where they translate into energy for the cow.

While the process happens, the cows power down for a few hours.

I know I've mentioned a little bit about how a cow's stomach works, but let me get a little more detailed. One of the most common questions I hear when kids tour the farm is, "Do cows really have four stomachs?"

And then I roll my eyes and yell "Scram!" and tell the kid to go to the back of the line.

That's another joke, people.

I fancy myself to be The Harbinger of Truth, so here's a quick explanation of how a cow's ONE—that's right: one—stomach works.

To give you an analogy, think about your own heart. The human heart has four chambers; the left and right atria, and the left and right ventricles. However, you only have one heart.

Got it? One lone, single heart divided into four chambers.

Same deal with a cow's stomach. One single stomach divided into four chambers.

When a cow eats, they first swallow the food into the first chamber of the stomach called the rumen. If you have ever watched closely while a cow grazes, you'll see that they rip up a hunk of grass and then swallow it whole. It's the same with their feed. They shovel up a mouthful and send it straight down the hatch.

The rumen acts like a filter for the food. A very small portion of the food product, and much of the moisture or water, is already broken down well enough that it can pass through the filter. Most of it, however, stays in the rumen to begin digestion.

Our human stomachs have a lot of acid in them. Ask anyone with a stomach ulcer how powerful stomach acid can be. The acid, mixed with a little bile, breaks down our food effectively since we have a pretty diverse diet. We need a powerful acid because we are omnivores; we can eat almost anything, whether it be plant or animal. Cows, on the other hand, exclusively eat plant cellulose. Their stomach specializes in breaking down this single type of food.

The rumen does not contain acid. Instead, it is chock-full of bacteria that go to work breaking down all of that harsh, fibrous cellulose. Humans do not have an abundance of these specialized bacteria; therefore we do not break down fiber very well. That's why a good bran muffin every morning helps you to keep traffic moving on the freeway, if you know what I mean. The fiber does not break down, so it acts like my tractor scraper in the barn; it barrels through your digestive system intact, grabbing, pushing, and pulling everything else along with it. The net result is you sitting on the throne the next morning, reading a newspaper while the fiber rediscovers a little daylight.

I'm sure I ought to be sorry for all these colorful epithets. But, I'm not.

The cows do have the bacteria to take care of the fiber. They fill the rumen, then go plop down next to a shade tree while the rest of their digestive process goes to work. Cellulose breaks down over time, and their food can now pass through the filter and into the reticulum, the second chamber of the stomach.

The cow will also help the bacteria break down the fibers by chewing tem. Once under the shade tree, the cow burps up her food and chews it. Remember that she didn't chew it in the first place? Now she does, a little bit at a time. That's called rumination, or "chewing cud" in the vernacular. Cows chew their food for the exact same reason humans chew our food: to break it down even further. That way, they can begin to absorb nutrients from the food. This takes place in the third chamber of the stomach: the omasum.

The omasum acts like a giant sponge. Its primary function is to pull water from the food. The tissue that makes up the omasum also begins to pull a small amount of nutrients, but it is working hard to absorb water and send it immediately to the rest of the body. Food doesn't spend a lot of time in the omasum before it gets moved into the final chamber, the abomasums.

At long last, we can talk about the cow's stomach in human terms, because the abomosum works almost exactly like a human stomach. This is where the acid and the bile live. The remaining materials are dissolved down to where their nutrients can be separated and extracted, both in the abomosum and during their journey through the intestines.

If you ever find yourself curious enough to examine a pile of cow manure, notice how smooth it is. Their diet consists of nothing but hard grains and fibrous grasses, and yet their poop is like soft-serve ice cream.

You might not want to repeat that to your kids.

Compare that poop to a horse's poop. When you examine "horse apples," you can actually see strands of hay poking out, thereby creating a pile of stinky sea urchins. It's much like human poop—if you eat corn kernels, you will likely see corn in your stool the next day. Or, if you eat peanuts, your stool will have chewed up, but undigested, little shards of peanut in it. It's not pretty, but it happens.

If you don't have any easy access to either horse or cow poop, I suggest checking out the nifty photos of each in a cool blog post, "How Does Your Cow's Stomach Really Work?" by Shelby DeVore. The blog is called Farminence, and you can access those photos at farminence.com/cows-stomach.

Why the difference? Because horses and humans do not have those bacteria, nor do we have a four-chambered stomach system that breaks down fiber. Cow stomachs are perfectly evolved digestive machines.

Digestion requires energy. Cows need four times the stomach power as humans to complete the digestive process, therefore they spend a lot of time lying around, conserving energy.

***

Cows rest for about 14 hours each day. This comes hot on the heels of spending somewhere between three and five hours each day eating and drinking. Once again, they eat and drink a lot, which requires time. Cows also naturally exercise themselves. According to Erin Brown (n.d.), cows spend about two to three hours each day walking around.

Cows are all rather subdued, from an aggression and personality standpoint. Most species of animals (humans included) engage in some sort of play. Typically, the way an animal plays is related to the development of survival skills. Dogs wrestle with each other, thereby practicing fighting skills. Cats hunt and chase toys (or any available string), sharpening skills that would serve them to find food in the wild. Humans play games developing competitive skills, learning rule-based behavior, and fostering critical thinking. Some humans will take care of dolls or stuffed animals, practicing parenting and nurturing skills. Others will build things and crash things, learning mechanics and developing visual/special skills.

Yet, cows don't really "play." They may assert dominance over each other by tussling a little bit. They'll head butt each other like mountain goats. It's interesting to watch.

In many social groups, a stratum will evolve. Some will assume natural leadership roles and some become followers. Many social animals have a dominance hierarchy when they interact. It's how they maintain stability and efficacy within the social group. If a social group has no leader, the group becomes ineffective. Having no natural leadership will dampen the group's cohesion and motivation. They may feel disorganized and directionless (Rowell, 1974).

Cows get along with an understanding of who the dominant one is. Story, one of my favorite cows in the current herd, is a dominant cow. She will pick on other cows to establish her dominance. However, when it comes to the true leader of the herd, then that's me. Story keeps a wary eye on me as she grapples with our roles in the herd. It's my voice that all the cows hear. They know I give direction, and they respond. I am the one who feeds and waters them, so they have learned over time that I am the ultimate leader of the herd.

Francie, on the other hand, is more of a submissive. She is constantly in my back pocket. She'll follow me around and engage in playful activity.

You've all been around an animal when it wants attention. A dog will shove its head under your hand, or a cat will rub herself on your legs when they want to be petted. Francie does a version of that behavior; a version that is only possible with a half a ton beast. She will put her head under my butt while I walk and lift me off my feet.

I'm sure she finds this to be uproariously funny; it definitely gets my attention. She does it to say that she wants me to scratch her head or her neck, providing simple contact that comforts her.

Oddly…Jersey cows need a certain number of minutes each day to devote to playing with their tongues. This sounds like a joke, but it's only halfway a joke. They really do play with their tongues more than any other breed of cow I have ever been around. They twirl them, flick them, and can lick their way through solid wood. Watch them while they are in repose in a pasture. I guarantee those tongues will be active.

When it comes to play and leisure, much of my herd also enjoys the cow brush—although that might be more related to scratching an itch than actual play. Cows get itchy and have a rough hide, so the brush will massage them while providing the friction that hits the spot.

Cows are extremely docile. It takes a lot to irritate a dairy cow. Beef cows are more feral in this respect; they are closer to their free-range ancestors than dairy cattle. Beef cows are more likely to trample or head-butt in an aggressive manner. Dairy cows would require a lot of provocation before they ever got near the point of lashing out.

Added together, all these activities account for nearly 22 hours of every day. The remaining two-ish hours are spent doing maintenance and management activities. It only takes about ten minutes to milk a cow with our machines, so they get milked twice per day, accounting for about 20 total minutes. They may also have health maintenance during that time (breeding, calving, veterinarian check-ups, etc.). Or they may do something that fascinates viewers on Facebook: get their hooves trimmed.

***

I'm not sure why people get transfixed on certain videos. Once in a while, I'll post one that I know is going to be a smash hit...and it fizzles. On the other hand, there are a handful videos that seem mundane to me, but they take off to over a millions views. The hoof trimming video is one that cleared the one million mark. I'll give a quick explanation for those of you who may not have seen it.

Everyone knows what horseshoes are. Of course, before the backyard game was ever invented, the shoes served a real purpose. They protect a horse's feet (hooves) from wear and tear, much like a pair of shoes protects your feet from injury. Hooves are made from similar material as your finger and toenails. While harder than skin, they are not above getting broken, infected, or worn down to the point of exposing vulnerable flesh. Hence, crescent-shaped shoes for horses are either forged from metal or made from high-tech synthetic materials.

Fitting and installing horseshoes is an occupation in and of itself. A specialist called a farrier is responsible for the care and maintenance of the horse's feet; they are part blacksmith and part veterinarian. When they work on a horse, they remove the old set of shoes, prepare the hooves, assess any issues that need to be checked out by the farmer and/or veterinarian, and then fit a new set of shoes. They also balance the hooves, thereby making sure that each of the horse's legs ends up being the same length.

Bringing this concept into the world of cows, the same procedure is followed, only without the shoe part. Dairy cows spend their days lying around on the grass, not transporting a cowboy or a covered wagon across the open rocky terrain of Montana.

A caveat: Everything I know about horses comes from watching Gunsmoke.

My cows have no opportunity to wear down their hooves. Therefore, they do not need shoes, but their hooves still need regular maintenance.

Hooves grow continuously throughout the life of a cow, similar to how fingernails grow continuously throughout the life of a human. We feed our cows well, so their healthy diet lends itself to their body working efficiently, and thus, their hooves growing quickly. A visit to the spa for a mani-pedi can resolve this issue, while treating my cows to the posh lifestyle to which they have grown accustomed.

Jerseys have such long, beautiful eyelashes, so they'll also have some lash extensions put in, and maybe a touch of mascara applied at the spa.

I'm kidding!

Sheesh.

I have a guy in town who is the hoof guru. He visits the farm regularly, since each cow must get their hooves checked and cleaned up twice per year. When my guy spends the day on the farm, he is able to take care of 40-50 cows, depending upon how much work each cow needs and how cooperative all the cows are.

Some cows need very little work; their hooves remain dainty models of keratin perfection. Other cows have hooves that grow until they look like a cross between Freddie Krueger and a rocky outcropping in the Garden of the Gods in Colorado Springs, CO. Likewise, some cows have an easier time getting in and out of the harness than others. Some are cranky, some haven't had a chance for their coffee to soak in; you can identify with that.

If you do the math, the hoof guru spends roughly twenty days total on our farm, which equates to approximately one month of weekdays. Once my herd reaches 1,000 cows, my hoof guru will bump that to approximately 40 days on the farm per year.

Business is good in Tilamook.

Just to give you a heads-up: He probably trims hooves for a living so he can make…

(wait for it)…

A PROFIT!

I mean, what's with that?

When he arrives, we assemble the cows that are earmarked to get their hooves taken care of that day. One by one, they are walked to a specialized chute that is used exclusively for hoof-trimming.

This is actually a part that people have the most trouble with; the chute looks a little like a medieval torture device. In actuality, it is not all that uncomfortable for the cow. Yes, it is more restrictive than allowing them to roam free and nap in the shade, but it is a necessary tool. Without the chute to secure them snugly in place, their hooves would be nearly impossible for the hoof guru to trim. Their hooves would grow until they broke and then possibly contract an infection.

If you've ever told your kid to finish their vegetables, or had them get a measles booster at the pediatrician's office, it's the same feeling. Sometimes we have to do things we don't like because it is better for us than if we don't do it at all.

The cow gets walked into the chute and held in place by a locking gate. Once inside, they are lifted slightly off their feet by a harness under their chest.

It's similar to a car lift or a floor lift at the mechanic's shop. When the mechanic is working on your brakes, he or she doesn't want to have to crouch or bend down the entire time. Think how difficult it can be to change a tire on the side of the road. The little scissors jack that comes with the car only lifts the car a few inches off the ground. You end up kneeling on the asphalt to deal with the lug nuts and the tire removal/replacement. In the mechanic's garage, the car lift elevates the entire car until the tire and brake area is roughly chest high to the mechanic. They can then stand comfortably while working on your brakes.

The cows get lifted so the hoof guru doesn't have to work in a prone position all day long. We bring the cow hooves up to him, so to speak.

Then, one by one, the cow's feet are placed in stirrups and angled so their hoof faces the ceiling instead of the floor. Never fear; there's a joint there to help the leg bend, just like your wrist. We don't "over-bed" the cow's wrists; we take advantage of their natural range of motion.

First order of business: assess each hoof. Not only is the hoof guru sizing up how much work needs to be done on the hoof, but he is also looking for damage or disease.

Once the cow is harnessed and their leg is lifted toward the hoof guru, the real fun begins. Interestingly, this part of the process is the most aggressive, in terms of sound and spectacle, but most people don't seem to have a problem with it. Oh, don't get me wrong; they cringe. But I think everyone understands that trimming fingernails is necessary. So it stands to reason that trimming hooves is also necessary.

You may use a clipper to trim your nails. If you go to a nail salon to get a manicure, they'll use an emery board or a nail file to do a low-grade grinding in order to smooth the nails' edge.

Same with cows. Sort of. Instead of a clipper and an emery board, the hoof guru uses an angle grinder. Before you ask, the answer is "yes." It's not a special "hoof guru tool" that he special orders from a defense contractor in Nevada. Instead, he bops down to the hardware store, strolls to the power-tool aisle, and pulls an angle grinder right off the shelf.

Watching him work the grinder on a hoof is an interesting deal. But, once you've seen it 10,000 times, it loses some of its luster. But, I get it. I understand why people are fascinated by the video.

The hoof guru has done this so many times, it's now just a matter of muscle memory for him. He pays attention to what he's doing, but his hands work fast. The hooves are cleaned up with the speed and grace of Michelle Kwan completing a flawless triple-axle on the ice.

Zip, zip, zip—shards of ground-up hoof fly through the air. Then, BAM—he's done, and on to the next hoof. The cow doesn't feel a thing. Just like you clipping your nails.

When he finishes all four feet, the cow is lowered to the ground and released from the chute. We walk the next cow in and do it all again. I make it sound easy, but it's difficult, physical work. I am grateful to have the hoof guru. I would have to do it myself if there wasn't a guy in town I trusted. As you can imagine, it's a lot easier to outsource the job to a professional who does this all day every day. He makes it look easy.

That's not the only part of the bovine mani-pedi. We help to maintain hoof health by running every cow through a foot bath after each milking. The hoof bath is placed in the return lane that every cow follows to get back to the barn after milking. It's a simpler process than you may imagine. The cows don't have to sit in a hot tub for twenty minutes, reading the paper and complaining about politics. Instead, they merely walk through a puddle-deep solution of a specialized copper sulfate-based wash designed to keep their hooves hard. The solution also helps to prevent hoof-related diseases, like hoof rot, hairy warts, and abscesses. Those are incredibly nasty. Despite what the activists say, we don't want our cows to deal with anything awful like that.

In our new facility, we will have a foaming foot bath installed. The hoof-hardening and anti-microbial solution will foam up around the feet of each cow walking through it. The foaming action actually cuts down on chemical usage and waste. It's a more ideal process with regard to sustainability.

***

By and large, that's really what cows do all day. Almost every day of the year is exactly the same for them. The exceptional days are when they are bred, which only takes about one minute, or when they calf, which will alter their routine for a few days at most. There's the occasional vet check-up, and the possibility of getting some intravenous medicine if they get sick. All in all, they live a predictably predictable life.

How's that for some tautology?

Chapter 13
Should We Drink Milk?

Let's talk about why we drink milk. A common anthem among activists is that humans shouldn't be drinking milk in the first place. Allow me to set the record straight and give a brief history of the relationship between milk and mankind.

Milk is important in our lives. From a nutritional standpoint, milk is an excellent source of protein, calcium, and 13 vitamins. From a financial standpoint, it provides a solid bang for your buck. From a taste standpoint, it is sweet and smooth and mixes well with any number of flavorings and recipes. And from a historical standpoint, it has been critical in the survival of our species, particularly in Northern countries, where winter sunlight is sparse.

The activists are quick to point out that humans are the only species that drink the milk of a different species. They use that idea to back up their main gripe: that human beings don't need cow milk to survive.

To give the activists their due, the first point is semi-true and the second point is completely true. However, that doesn't mean they are related to each other; nor are they relevant. Yes, we are the only mammals that drink the milk of other species. Cats drink cream, but only because you put it in a bowl on the floor. It's really not a good idea to give them a lot of milk, anyway; they are lactose intolerant. From an evolutionary standpoint, marauding hordes of tabbies and Persians have never terrorized the land, fiercely seizing cattle and soaking in the milk of their udders.

There are a few species of birds that steal milk from mammals. The red-tailed oxpecker will steal milk from the teats of impalas. Seagulls and sheathbills steal from nursing elephant seals. And, back in the 1920s in England, blue tits learned how to peck through the thin aluminum foil tabs on top of milk when it was delivered to the doorstep (Green, 2017; Kanchwala, 2021).

So the activists are almost correct on one point. Regarding our need to drink milk, of course we don't need to. Plenty of people are lactose intolerant and skip animal milk altogether. They live happy and healthy lives. Plenty of vegans think they're doing animals a favor by not eating meat or drinking milk, but their efforts are sadly misguided. We drink milk because we like it and because it is a super food.

***

It is often explained to me by online vegans (virtue signaling as always) that they are never going to use a single animal product ever, Ever, EVER. Therefore, they are not going to eat meat or consume dairy. I reply to them that there are way more things besides food in modern society that come from animals. Stuff you may not even realize and probably can't live without.

Yes, I conceded the fact that we are the only species of mammal that drinks milk produced by another species. If I'm not mistaken, I believe we are also the only species of mammal that drives cars. Therefore, should we give up the automobile as well?

Sometimes, they come back with a counterpoint: "Yeah, but cars don't require you to kill animals because they don't use animal by-products."

I say "Oh, yes they do."

For all my vegan friends (I probably have one somewhere out there), here is a brief list of things in your world that come directly from the animals you think you are protecting. For the record, this list is in no way exhaustive. You can look online for staggering lists of thousands of products that use some part of an animal to produce.

I'll start with cows because, well...I shouldn't have to explain that one. Aside from delicious and nutritious meat and dairy foods, cow by-products are almost ubiquitous in our society. For example, tallow is the fat from cattle and is used in crayons, paints, soap, lipstick, shaving cream, candles, and rubber. How many things in your home right now have rubber in them?

When you boil a cows' skin, tendons, and bones, you extract a protein called gelatin. Cows aren't the only animals we get gelatin from, so bear that in mind when you try to convince yourself you are completely vegan. Gelatin is used in shampoo, cosmetics, candy, marshmallows, and of course, Jell-O and pudding.

Cow hide becomes one of the most prevalent fabrics in use: leather. Again, cows aren't the only animals from which we obtain leather, but they are the primary contributors. Vegans do their best to avoid leather, but it is everywhere from clothes to furniture to shoes to purses. Even if you don't have leather furniture in your home or leather seats in your car, I guarantee your fanny has touched a leather seat somewhere along the way.

For shame!

I'll include the humble pig into this discussion because I don't want to bore you with an exhaustive list of how many animal by-

166

products are embedded in the world around you. Not only are pigs the most widely eaten animal on earth, but products made from pigs are completely entrenched in the way we live our lives in the modern world.

It may surprise you to know that insulin, heart valves, and gelatin to make drug capsules can come from pigs. The medical field has used pig parts for decades when treating humans.

Other pig body parts are used in making rubber, antifreeze, chalk, adhesives, film for your camera, pet food, and industrial lubricants, which are required to run machines that make thousands of other products.

It is impossible to live a truly vegan lifestyle, short of going completely caveman or "Naked and Afraid." However, hunting and fishing seem to be common survival strategies for both the contestants and the cavemen.

Weird, right?

I encourage everyone to check out the website www.animalsmart. org/feeding-the-world/products-from-animals. Don't let the kid-friendly interface put you off; this site is run by the American Society of Animal Science. They list hundreds of products made from all kinds of animals, including horses, goats, rabbits, fish, chickens, sheep, and bees. You'll be amazed how many aspects of life animals touch.

***

Evolution and nature are pretty good at knowing what to do. Milk is produced by every female mammal to feed to their newborns. I believe there have been trillions upon trillions (maybe more?) of mammals throughout the entire history of time that have survived infancy solely through the nutrition of their mother's milk.

I would like to share a well-written essay that was forwarded to me by Stacy Foster, the Senior Manager of Industry Relations and Communications for the Oregon Dairy and Nutrition Council. The essay was written by a graduate student, Tim Pierson, at The University of Utah for the Dairy Council of Utah/Nevada in 2014. Tim was nice enough to grant us full permission to reprint the article in its entirety.

While I tend to dislike long quoted material, I don't think I could have written a better article myself.

Milk: The History and Controversy

By Tim Pierson
Graduate Student, Division of Nutrition,
University of Utah

As a graduate student of nutrition, I often find myself heating up the kitchen of countless parties or

167

gatherings. Not because I am cooking up all kinds of delicious appetizers and hors d'oeuvres, but rather because I am talking to people about food - food trends, popular diets, food avoidances etc.And the conversation almost always whips around to the topic of milk.

Milk, although widely accepted by many around the world, seems to stir up passionate debates in every setting with demands like: "Should we drink milk?" "Is it safe?" "Raw, organic, or regular?" "Whole or skim?" "Almond, Soy, or Cow? Camel milk?"

All of these questions can be answered by taking a look at the history of milk; animal milk that is. It is a story that begins back at the dawn of agriculture, about 10,000 B.C.E. Cuneiform tablets indicate that ancient Near Easterners gave fresh milk to royalty, while the common milk—that which was soured from sitting out—was used to make butter and cheese. Romans historically offeredlibum, essentially the original cheesecake, to the gods. Fast forwarding to 14thcentury Europe, milk found its way to the top becoming the "white liquor," a necessary item for any respectable banquet or soiree. Milk (animal milk in general) was a prized possession for Europeans—some might even argue it still is—evidenced by the highly sought-after milk chocolate produced in the region.

However, the history of dairy consumption has not always been favorable. Physicians once advised individuals to consume cheese after a large meal to act as a kind of "plug" or "stopper" due to the constipation it caused some people. Likely the result of some intolerance and souring, many cultures viewed its consumption as barbaric and pungent.

You might ask yourself, "Why then, have we evolved to indulge in this white elixir? And should we even be drinking it?" The simple answer is yes, we should consume dairy. Here's a bit of history about why.

Northern Europeans evolved to tolerate lactose from the milk of domesticated animals thousands of years ago and benefited from its nutrition profile with longer life and healthier bones—the genes of those healthier individuals were passed on to future generations. At the time, people did not understand that it was milk's unique nutrient package, which includes calcium, protein, and naturally occurring vitamin D that was giving them a survival advantage, whilst preventing bone issues like rickets, but they knew that milk had its benefits and was contributing to a healthier, longer life.

To quote an 1893 article found in Hoard's Dairyman: "There is something about milk which is nearly impossible to replace, that stimulates assimilation and digestion and promotes growth."

They were onto something. And thanks to Elmer V. McCollum in 1920, vitamin A was discovered by looking at the fat from whole milk. This led to the discovery of vitamin D two years later.

Your skin, with sun exposure, manufactures Vitamin D—and there are few foods that contain naturally occurring vitamin D. Northern Europeans who had been drinking milk were getting a boost during the winter months—when there's not much sun up north—and the vitamin D found naturally in milk was helping to maintain bone integrity. Due to its importance, and because naturally occurring vitamin D can be inconsistent in the milk supply, the U.S. began fortifying milk with Vitamin D in the 1930's.

With what we have learned over the years about milk—cow's milk—from first the cultural and later nutritional standpoint, how can we deny the benefits and nutrients it provides? Of course which milk you choose to drink—whole, low-fat, skim, lactose-free, organic, raw, or regular—is entirely a personal decision. But it is one that can be made with the satisfaction of knowing that what you are getting is quality nutrition from hard working cows and farmers near you. Perhaps McCollum said it best: "There is no substitute for [cow's] milk, and its use should be distinctly increased instead of diminished, regardless of cost (Pierson, 2014)."

I love that stuff! We often think of milk in terms of calories and fats and proteins, but milk contains other important nutrients like calcium and Vitamins A and D. Plus, milk supplies us with:

Vitamin B12
Phosphorous
Riboflavin
Selenium
Potassium
Pantothenic acid
Thiamin
Zinc (Frey, 2021)

Much of this is above my pay grade; I'm just a lowly dairy farmer. But nutritionists will tell you that your body needs all kinds of vitamins and minerals to remain healthy; even some you've never heard of. Milk gives us a good dose of what we need. Every drop of milk, bovine and human alike, is dense with nutrients. For every 100 calories of milk consumed, you get so much for so little. It destroys the competition!

Don't take my word for it. Let the data speak for itself. I recommend Diana Rodgers, RD, LDN, at www.sustainabledish.com. She is a Licensed Registered Dietitian Nutritionist. She takes the time to fully educate people on all matters related to nutrition, backed by hard data and real science. She has a few books of her own out there, and does public speaking and podcasting. She's a great resource.

I also recommend Dr. Shawn Baker, the carnivore diet guy. You can find him at shawn-baker.com. He's a little more controversial, but he also backs up his claims with peer-reviewed scientific studies.

Please be a wary consumer and a very critical thinker when someone online claims to use "science." Look for a listing of sources, and then take a moment to check them out. The activists love to cherry pick little pieces of data, remove any context, and blow them up. I'd like to show examples of how this can be done.

I believe everyone is familiar with drowning deaths and car accidents.

I think everyone has heard different variations on how most drowning deaths take place close to the shore. A quick Google search reveals an interesting article on drowning deaths in Kauai, Hawaii, USA (Blay, 2018).The article appropriately cites data, noting that over the past 43 years, a whopping 76% of drowning deaths have occurred in the nearshore marine waters of the island.

At first blush, you might wonder if there is some inherent danger when you are close to the island.

Maybe riptides?

Maybe an underwater chasm?

Maybe a steep drop-off into the waiting tentacles of the Kraken?

But rather than contemplate this statistic at face value, ask yourself the most important contextual question: Where do most people swim when they are in Hawaii?

Sure, some people are swimming in hotel swimming pools. Some paddle a surfboard out past the nearshore waters. And some grab their fishing gear and go way out to sea on a boat. But the vast majority of people are splashing and playing and swimming near the shore. That's why the vast majority of drownings take place near the shore!

Once you realize that, you're like, "Well, no duh."

The same can be true with car accidents. Let's say that 52% of all vehicular accidents occur within a five-mile radius of the driver's home? If that is so, then 69% could occur within a ten-mile radius.

The same rules as drowning apply to this statistic. If roughly 70% of all car accidents happen within ten miles of home, is there something about where you live that makes driving more dangerous than in the neighboring town?

No.

Where do you drive the most? It's normally within ten miles of your house; running kids to school, going to the grocery store, attending church on Sunday. All of these trips are within a short drive of your home. The more time you spend driving in a place, the more likely a car accident will take place there.

Simple context doesn't slant the statistics or the data. Rather, context slants your impression of the statistics or the data. What duplicitous activists will do is play an obfuscation game. One of their favorite tactics is to create official-sounding websites so they can push out medical-sounding information to befuddle unsuspecting consumers.

I'll give the example of one shell website that cherry-picks data. The organization itself has a very impressive sounding name: The Physicians Committee for Responsible Medicine (PCRM). Wouldn't you believe information that was underscored by something that sounds as official as the PCRM?

However, according to activistfacts.com, the PCRM is tied to fanatical animal rights groups. But don't just take our word for it. The same article on activistfacts.com cites Mary Carmichael in Newsweek magazine—a pretty good mainstream source for information—who noted that less than 5% of the members of PCRM are actually physicians (Carmichael, 2004). Carmichael goes on to write that the PCRM president, Neal Barnard, has been demonstrated to have ties to PETA (People for the Ethical Treatment of Animals), and an organization called Stop Huntingdon Animal Cruelty—an animal rights group the Department of Justice calls a "domestic terrorist threat,"(Activist Facts, n.d.).

Listen, don't just take my word for it. On anything I write. Be an informed consumer of information. Think about the source of the information—how credible is the source? Do I like the information because it matches my bias, or because it is legitimate? Is the author (or content creator) actually in the field they are talking about? Can I accept that there might be information that challenges my belief system?

Ask a farmer, not an activist. I live it every day, so I understand how dairy farming works. I am also open to accepting that cow milk is a very good food source.

Calves drink nothing but mother's milk when they are first born. This milk begins their journey to grow into 1,200 pound cows. During their infancy, they don't drink anything else, nor do they eat anything else. Mamma's milk is all their body needs during the most rapid growth period of their lifecycle.

***

Dairy farming has a huge problem among our ranks. Mental health issues are rampant among farmers, and the data is quite shocking.

In 2018, an article about a research paper was put together by agriculture communication students and their faculty mentor, Dr. Scott Vernon at Cal Poly San Luis Obispo. In it, the authors cited Centers for Disease Control data on suicide in the agricultural industry (Fitchette, 2018). The brief article made the rounds among farmers, many of whom nodded silently while reading it over. To everyone outside of our industry, this may come as quite a surprise because nobody talks about it.

At the top of their data list was perhaps the most jarring statistic: farmers have the highest rate of suicide among any occupation (84.5 per 100,000 agriculture workers) (Fitchette, 2018).

Can you believe that?

I can.

We often hear about health care workers or cops when it comes to high suicide rates. Believe me, I totally understand how those could be stressful and thankless occupations as well. However, I don't know that I have ever heard anyone refer to how many farmers commit suicide. The reason might be related to their second point made in the article.

Many farm deaths are reported as accidents rather than suicides (Fitchette, 2018). This matter takes a little more depth to completely break it down. The point made by the authors is that suicide rates might actually be higher than reported because some (a few? several? many?) of the "accidental" deaths might actually be suicides in disguise.

I get that not all of those accidents were suicides. Farming is a dangerous game to play. There is good reason that the "farming accident" is a bit of a cliché. We work around giant animals, large machinery, and sharp whirling objects year round. Accidents happen, with most resulting in injury rather than death. Thank goodness.

But the availability of so many options could give a suicidal farmer a chance to end their pain in the line of duty. I'm not morose enough to think a desperate farmer might want to "make it look like an accident" in order to protect the family life insurance policy, although that is certainly a possibility. What I mean is that farmers see danger every day. These dangers might open an avenue for their anguished mind to exploit.

There is also the possibility of a half-accident. Depression causes a person to lose focus. If you aren't concentrating, you could easily fall prey to a giant animal or a large machine. Whether by accident or on purpose, the incident is driven by the farmer's underlying mental state.

Incidentally, the authors duly note that several big farming states were not included in the CDC farm suicide data: California, Illinois, Iowa and Nebraska. Anyone who has driven through the Midwest can attest to the enormity of the farming community in Illinois, Iowa, and Nebraska. People don't generally think of California when they think of farming, probably because Cali doesn't have a lot of corn. But there are a lot of farmers in California, particularly in the northern half of the state Therefore, the numbers are most likely even higher than the ones reported.

And that is scary, folks.

The concluding point made by the research paper was that suicide rates today are about 50 percent higher than they were during the farming crisis of the 1980s (Fitchette, 2018). It seems that farmers are struggling more now than ever before. Since the 1980s, the problems seem to be getting worse. Why is that?

I don't need a research paper or a college professor or a scientist at the CDC to point out the pressure points experienced by a farmer. I experience them every day.

To begin, there isn't a lot of money in farming. Despite what the activists tell you about greedy farmers squeezing every nickel out of the consumer in order to extract society's wealth, many farmers swim pretty hard to keep their head above the water.

Land is the great limiter. There is only so much that can be produced by either crop or livestock per acre. Because a farmer can't just snap their fingers and make more land magically appear, we are constantly at the mercy of market trends when we sell our products. That's what happened in an accelerated way in the 1980s. The ag market crashed, leaving farmers with no place to sell what they had produced.

The ebb and flow of the market is extremely stressful, which is why I appreciate the Tillamook co-op so much. They control pricing rather well, giving us some predictability when selling our milk.

Also, we work around family. Farms are handed down from one generation to the next, with most family members living on the same parcel of land as their parents and/or grandparents. This has been changing within the last couple generations, as many younger people are choosing to leave the farm and find other career paths because of the money issue. But for hundreds, or possibly thousands, of years, farming was a family business.

It is certainly the case here at Wilsonview. I represent the fourth generation of Josis that have run our farm. Frankly, I don't even know how far "the farm" extends back into the motherland. My great-grandfather started our farm in the location I still farm today, but his father was a farmer back in Switzerland. I have no idea how many generations worked that land before great-gramps relocated to the United States.

It can be difficult to work around family members seven days a week. My dad and I get along very well, but we get annoyed at each other all the time. We both have big personalities and both think we know what's best. Dad has been a farmer all his life, just as I have (for the most part). When we butt heads, we go to our neutral corners and work it out internally, then reconvene later in the day.

We have to get along because we have to work together to keep the farm going. That's not always as simple as it sounds. Thankfully, Dad and I have a good rhythm. My favorite part of the week is Sunday morning. On Sundays, only Dad and I are on the farm. There are no workers present; it's quiet. Sure, we have more to do because we have no help, but we relax and work together.

The other problem inherent to working with and around family all the time is that you have very few options when it comes to "Who can I complain to?" The very people irritating you are the ones you are around almost 24/7. There isn't a lot of opportunity to talk it out. Hence, we remain trapped in our heads until we can process the irritation and work it through.

Lastly, farmers have a few factors unique to them that make mental health issues difficult to deal with.

Farmers tend to be isolated. Particularly on bigger farms, the land encompasses a wide berth around the home. We have approximately 400 acres here at Wilsonview. My family lives on one part of the property and my parents live on another part. As you can imagine, our closest neighbors are probably a fair distance further away than your neighbors. There aren't a lot of "chatting over the back fence" conversations happening in my neighborhood. We don't see many people off the farm during the work day.

We don't have a lot of time to seek mental health services. My job requires me to work every day of the year. Dairy cows require attention every twelve hours; they have to get milked and fed. Automation has cut our workload significantly, but we are still required to interact with the cows during both of those shifts.

Plus, we have dozens of chores to stay on top of. Maintenance of the infrastructure, meetings with auditors and inspectors, veterinary / health checks, and running off to tamp down whatever random crisis emerges at any given time, night or day, are all a part of the job description. It is enormously stressful. Unfortunately, we eat it and smile.

If we don't do what needs to be done, no one else will.

Finally, there is the overall stigma of mental health issues themselves. I have been around farmers my whole life. Believe me when I say that farmers don't tend to be Chatty Cathies in the first place. But deep, innermost thoughts are never bandied about around the coffee pot at the co-op. Yet, other farmers are the only ones who can truly understand our lifestyle. It's difficult to find a therapist who is up-to-speed on farming. At least, enough so they can make a farmer feel comfortable.

The predominant shared characteristic in farmers is strength, both physical and mental. Our job is quite physical, although machines and automation have reduced the physical strain considerably over the past century. One thing machines cannot take away is the need to remain mentally strong. We have no choice when we are confronted with life-and-death decisions regarding our herd. There is nobody behind me; I am the last line of defense at Wilsonview. If something is happening with a cow, from tough calving to euthanasia to a serious injury, I am the one who ultimately has to make a decision and then act upon it.

Plus, I am the final say when it comes to any big changes with the farm. There can be tens of thousands of dollars at stake with almost every change I make. That is a lot of pressure. If the changes go well, I am satisfied in knowing I made a good choice. If the changes fail or cause us to lose money, I sit alone with the knowledge that I erred.

They say it's lonely at the top. That sounds cliché, but I totally get it.

If a farmer is feeling stress, they put their head down and keep working. If they are feeling overwhelmed or depressed, they put their head down and keep working. If they are having trouble at home (marital problems, kids getting in trouble at school, etc.), they put their heads down and keep working.

It's the way we have all been taught to think and proceed. Ignore the pressure; ignore your distress. You are in charge of the family and the farm; it's up to you to keep it afloat.

And listen, every farmer understands these issues. Most handle it pretty well. Speaking for myself, I have personally dealt with a mental health issue and personal therapy.

I didn't think it was a major crisis, but I could feel the boat rocking. I wanted some help to sort it out before my life took on too much water. I needed an outside voice to give me tools to handle stress. I was young and under a lot of pressure. I didn't always make the best choices. The therapist was an asset. I still incorporate some of the tools I learned in my current life.

So, it's true. I'm no stranger to the stresses and strains of balancing home and work. Even as I write this book in 2021, I have days where the alarm goes off at 2:30am and I don't want to get out of bed.

But I do get out of bed. And I'm okay. I have a GREAT wife, who helps to keep me sane and stable. I have four great kids who fill me with pride and joy. And I have a supportive extended family that shares the burden when I need a minute to recharge.

So hug a farmer, everyone!

That may have sounded weird. But, I'm sticking to it.

In all seriousness, for farmers reading this book and for anyone who knows a farmer—make sure everyone stays healthy. There are more services available today than there were even a few years ago because of technology. You can visit a counselor online so that you don't even have to leave the farm (even though you might like to get away for a couple hours every week). Even psychiatric visits can be done virtually. If you aren't good with computers, I'm sure you know someone who can assist in the navigation.

The industry is shrinking. I think I heard somewhere that the average age of farmers in the United States is 62 years old. I don't know if that's entirely accurate, but it seems true enough for me. We need all the farmers we can get.

So, please take care of yourselves.

Chapter 14
Answering the Burning Questions

Alright. Before I wrap this up, let me address two questions I get asked with some regularity. In fact, one of them cracks me up. Because when I Google my name, it is one of the top related searches: "Has Derrick Josi been married before?"

I had no idea people were curious about something that has very little to do with anything, but to each his own, I suppose.

The other topic people love to ask about is how Kaycee and I met. Origin stories can be cute, and ours is no exception. So, here are the answers to those burning questions.

***

My oldest two children (my son, Bryson and my daughter, Addison) are from my first marriage, which lasted from the time I was 21 years old until the time I was about 28. I rarely talk about my divorce because I don't want my children to think any less of either parent. I will say that we were both young—probably too young to consider being married for the rest of our lives. But we are blessed with two precious kids from the union. I wouldn't trade any of my kids for the moon, so I have a hard time looking back upon my first marriage with any bitterness or resentment.

My general advice for young people is to not get married and have kids until they are at least 30 years old. Your twenties are meant for you to live life and have a good time. Make sure you get everything out of your system and have the maturity to make better decisions once you choose your life partner.

Nobody listens to an old dairy farmer giving out relationship advice, but I stand by my wisdom.

I know. I didn't give very much info. As for the rest of the story: none of your beeswax. You got your answer in no uncertain terms. And as Forrest Gump was fond of saying, "That's all I'm gonna say about that."

Instead, I'll tell a story about how a boy met a girl.

Honestly, it's about how a pretty awesome boy met an even awesomer girl.

Most people who follow me on social media are familiar with my family. I sometimes struggle with deciding how much or how little to include the younger kids in the social media marketing game. On one hand, I don't say much about the older kids because I want to protect them. They are 14 and 13 years old respectively (as of this writing), and are already at an age replete with inter- and intra-personal struggles, especially as social media pervades their lives.

The younger kids don't have quite that angst yet, but I do wonder if I will pare back the amount of information I share as they get older. For now, they are a hit and universally welcomed by folks on Facebook, Twitter, and Instagram.

My wife is Kaycee, and with her I have been able to make some changes with regard to who I am as a partner. I learned a lot about myself and about life while going through my divorce. Kaycee gives me a chance to be a better husband, father, and man.

Our origin story might make me look bad, but I'll tell it anyway.

***

I didn't know Kaycee before we started dating. Somewhat fortuitously, her Aunt Charlotte used to do milk testing for our family farm. Auntie evidently saw something in me that she thought would be a good fit for her niece.

I have no idea what she could have seen. Following my divorce, I made quite a few bad choices with regard to dating. I lost a little dignity along the way, until I finally reached a point where I was ready to find a good companion with whom to settle down and start another version of my life.

Aunt Charlotte kept telling me about this niece of hers who lived over in Canby, a small town about two hours east of our farm. She went on and on about how we should meet, how I'd really like her, how she thought we'd be a good couple, among many things.

Little did I know, Aunt Charlotte was doing the exact same thing to Kaycee. By the time we met, Kaycee knew all about me through her aunt's persistent match-maker tendencies. However, unlike me, a crazy dating dude who probably seemed like he was always up for having a date with somebody's cute niece, Kaycee was like, "No! Not interested."

I was recently divorced and had two children. I'm also seven years older than her. I wasn't exactly the dreamy fantasy dude of a sane, 22 year-old single woman with options.

I was also hesitant.

What if this Kaycee gal was crazy and it ended badly?

Or if she boiled my bunny?

Or told all my friends I was a University of Oregon Ducks fan?

What then? Hmm? What then!?

She also lived two hours away. Why would I need that kind of aggravation in my life?

Hard pass. There was no way I was going to go through with that.

But, I went through with it.

Not completely blind, mind you. I had her vetted first. I went to a source I assumed would be reliable—my friend Gene from grade school.

Charlotte's daughter was married to Gene, so I asked him about Kaycee.

He vouched for her.

"Yeah...she's pretty cool." (Gene is a man of few words).

Then, he set the hook, "Next time she's in Tillamook, I'll text you and you can come out and meet her."

Cut away to a few weeks later. My phone buzzed. It was Gene. This was "the text."

He mentioned he was at a local bar, The Schooner, and that Kaycee was in town.

Furthermore, she was at The Schooner with him.

I raised an eyebrow. How bad could she be?

Boosted by bravado, away I went.

I met Kaycee Hoffman, and introduced myself with a fist bump. And who said chivalry is dead?

She was truly amazing. So much so, that I was late to work the next morning.

I had a great time with her. A PG-13 great time, mind you. She wasn't that kind of girl, which was important to me. We talked deep into the night. In fact, we were still talking when the vibe was interrupted by my phone ringing at three in the morning.

It was my dad. And he was not happy.

I gave him the bare bones of what he needed to know.

"Uh...yeah...I'm in Netarts, so it'll be about twenty minutes."

He wasn't pleased because it was already three in the morning.

I wasn't pleased because it was already three in the morning! Where did the time go? The time had flown by.

It was a long and sleepless night for me, but there was something special about Kaycee.

I broke all the dating rules because I messaged her the very next day. I couldn't help it. I had to! It seems like a cliché from any Hollywood rom-com to say she stood out from all the other girls I had known. But she really did!

The following week, I also drove to Canby to see her, which was two hours away. My version of "playing hard to get" was probably not well-executed.

Believe it or not, I made that drive a lot for the next year of my life.

A. LOT.

The three days each week that I didn't have my kids, I drove to Canby after work. And then I would drive home at one in the morning so I could arrive at work by three a.m.

It was a four-hour round trip, three days per week, with almost zero sleep on each of those days. That was my life. And she was worth it.

I'm not a sappy romantic; I'm a farmer. Kaycee felt like a perfect match for me. I was not about to ease up on the throttle and let her get away. I put 50,000 miles on my truck that year. It was a heck of a commute for a heck of a gal.

***

Forgive me for bragging on my wife for a moment. Kaycee was an amazing college athlete, and she deserves some props. She played softball for the Montana State Billings Yellowjackets in 2010 and 2011. To this day, she still holds the single season school record for on-base percentage (.449). If you aren't a softball fan, that means Kaycee reached base safely roughly one out of every two times she stepped up to the plate that year.

Her career .364 batting average ranks fourth all-time on the team. She also hit 23 home runs as a Yellowjacket. Considering she was only on the squad for two years, that number still ranks eighth all-time in school history. Nearly every girl above her played on the team a full four years. Kaycee's .670 lifetime slugging percentage still ranks second in school history.

In a nutshell, that is nothing short of amazing.

She is starting to help the girls around Tillamook with their hitting techniques. I'm extremely happy she's doing this because there is so much softball knowledge in her head. She tried coaching for a season, but small town politics were a bit overbearing for her taste. One-on-one sessions are much more to her liking.

***

A few years later, along came our daughter, Reagan. Her sister, Dylan, is the baby of the bunch. Based upon the projections given to us by the pediatrician, both girls are on course to top out over six feet tall. From a dad's perspective, that gives me some comfort. That could limit their dating pool (ha!). Plus, they have their mother's genes—so might pull down seven-figure salaries in the WNBA someday.

I'd like for them to foot the bill for Dad during his golden years.

I wouldn't say I have a favorite of the four kids. Although, come to think of it, that would keep all the kids on their toes. I will admit I get better and better at being a dad with each successive kid. I am a very good dad to Bryson and Addison. I was there when they were babies and toddlers too, but I worked a lot when they were younger. A lot.

I wish I would have spent more time with Bryson and Addison during that early time. But I am making up for it as we move along in life.

If you follow any of my videos on Facebook or Instagram, you can tell how important it is to me to be around my kids. A farmer's life is busy, unpredictable at times, and never stops. Still, I involve Reagan in most things I do. She's not in school yet, so she has the opportunity to spend these precious years around her dad while he's doing his job and making an income to support the family.

All in all, we lead a pretty good life.

Epilogue

So, that's the book, and them's my words.

I appreciate everyone who has enjoyed this journey with me. Not just the book itself, but to everyone who follows and shares what I do online. I may not love dairy farming every day of the year, but I love being a dairy farmer. I love working with the cows and generating a product that is consumed and enjoyed by so many millions of people.

Our farm was founded in 1912 and has been going strong ever since. In fact, we show no signs of slowing down. Quite the contrary; I am ramping up our enterprise so I can take care of more cows and serve more people.

I don't know when I will retire. Probably after Dylan has a chance to go to college and decide for herself what she would like to do with her life. That way, all four kids will have grown up and decided for themselves if they would like to keep the family farm alive.

I won't push that choice onto them. I will leave open the possibility for any, or all the kids who would like to take it on. If any of them want to step into my shoes, I will pass the farm to them just like my father passed it to me. And his father to him, and his father to him. If none of the kids want it, I'll sell the farm and help the new owner get into the groove before bowing out.

Either way, I'm going to retire someday. I don't believe I am one of those farmers who wants to get up at 2:30a.m. until the day I die. I want to travel a bit, spend time with my grandchildren, and continue to provide Kaycee with the life she wants to live.

Until that day, I will continue to fight the good fight and ward off online villains who are hell bent on taking down the dairy industry, and take me down personally. I step into that line of fire because I believe in what I do. I believe in the family business, but more importantly, I believe in the wholesome quality of the dairy products I produce.

So, please: tune in and watch the videos. You don't have to join the battle. You just have to listen and learn. And, maybe find some entertainment along the way. Sometimes I can be cranky, but it's only temporary. A lot like dairy farming, my battles online never cease.

I'm not a hero. I'm a farmer.

Author's Note

It seems appropriate to close this book by acknowledging a few people. First and most importantly, my wife, Kaycee, for her ability to support me when I come home with another project. Her patience with me and my crazy ideas is why I'm able to do what I do.

Steve Olivas needs a special acknowledgment because without him the crazy ideas and thoughts in my head would have stayed there. The many hours of conversation early in the morning are something I actually miss. We may have to write another book soon.

Just kidding Kaycee, but you never know.

Last, but not least, I'd like to say thank you to all those resources and people in the dairy industry who have supported this endeavor. Every single one of them helped get this book into your hands.

References

Activist Facts. (n.d.). Physicians committee for responsible medicine (PCRM). Retrieved from https://www.activistfacts.com/organizations/23-physicians-committee-for-responsible-medicine/

Agricultural Marketing Services. (2021, August 21). Retail Milk Prices Report (RMP Publication No. 0821). United States Department of Agriculture, Market Information Branch. Retrieved from https://www.ams.usda.gov/sites/default/files/media/RetailMilkPrices.pdf

Agricultural Marketing Services. (2020, June 22). National Organic Program: USDA Organic Regulation (Federal Register Publication No. 2020-09007). United States Department of Agriculture. Retrieved from https://www.federalregister.gov/documents/2020/05/07/2020-09007/national-organic-program-usda-organic-regulations

Allen, A. J. (2015). Parturient paresis in cows. MDS Manual Veterinary Manual. Kenilworth, NJ: Merk & Co., Inc. Retrieved from https://www.msdvetmanual.com/metabolic-disorders/disorders-of-calcium-metabolism/parturient-paresis-in-cows

Baker, M. (n.d.). Why barns are red and more paint color cues. This Old House. Retrieved from https://www.thisoldhouse.com/21015066/why-barns-are-red-and-more-paint-color-cues

Blay, C. (2018). Drowning deaths in Kauai ocean shoreline waters. The Edge of Kauai Investigations. Retrieved from https://www.teok.com/drowning-deaths-in-kauai-ocean-shoreline-waters/

Brown, C.M. & McLean, J.L. (2015). Anthropomorphizing dogs: projecting one's own personality and consequences for supporting animal rights. Anthrozoos, 28, 73-86.

Brown, E. (n.d.) A day in the life of a dairy cow [Web log post]. American Dairy Association Mideast. Retrieved from https://www.drink-milk.com/a-day-in-the-life-of-a-dairy-cow/

Boyle, D. (2018). 30-Second Great Inventions. London, U.K.: Ivy Press.

Can dairy be sustainable? Yes, and here's why. (2021, June 11). Undeniably Dairy News. Retrieved from https://www.usdairy.com/news-articles/dairy-farmers-advance-environmental-practices-get-results

Canola Council of Canada. (2021). Processing canola. In About Canola. Retrieved from https://www.canolacouncil.org/about-canola/processing/

Carmichael, M. (2004). Atkins Under Attack. Newsweek Magazine (February 22, 2004). Retrieved from https://www.newsweek.com/atkins-under-attack-131403

Chen, J. (2021). Fiat Money. In Investopedia Education Economy (September 9, 2021). Retrieved from https://www.investopedia.com/terms/f/fiatmoney.asp

Colorado Supreme Court. (2021, June 21). Ballot titles—single-subject requirement. In re: Title, Ballot Title & Submission Clause for 2021-2022, #16, No. 21SA. Retrieved from https://www.courts.state.co.us/userfiles/file/Court_Probation/Supreme_Court/Opinions/2021/21SA125.pdf

Conniff, R. (2009, August). The political history of cap and trade. Smithsonian Magazine. Retrieved from https://www.smithsonianmag.com/science-nature/the-political-history-of-cap-and-trade-34711212/

Corday, R. (2014, April 24). The evolution of assembly lines: a brief history. Robohub. Retrieved from https://robohub.org/the-evolution-of-assembly-lines-a-brief-history/

Cotton Counts. (n.d.). Cotton: from field to fabric. Retrieved from https://www.cotton.org/pubs/cottoncounts/fieldtofabric/upload/Cotton-From-Field-to-Fabric-129k-PDF.pdf

Custard, M.K. (2021). Understanding the Facebook algorithm in 2021: ranking signals and tips. AdEspresso by Hootsuite. Retrieved from https://adespresso.com/blog/facebook-algorithm/

Economic Research Service. (2014, January). Agricultural Act of 2014: Highlights and Implications [Chart]. Washington, D.C.: United States Department of Agriculture. Retrieved from https://www.ers.usda.gov/agricultural-act-of-2014-highlights-and-implications/

Espy, B. (2016). Equine reproduction from conception to birth. American Association of Equine Practitioners. Retrieved from https://aaep.org/horsehealth/equine-reproduction-conception-birth

FDAFinal Determination Regarding Partially Hydrogenated Oils, 80 FR 34650, at 34650-34670 (2015). Retrieved from https://www.federalregister.gov/documents/2015/06/17/2015-14883/final-determination-regarding-partially-hydrogenated-oils

Fitchette, R. (2018, June 7). Cal Poly San Luis Obispo Ag communications student tackle taboo topic in presentation to local farm leaders. Farm Progress. Retrieved from https://www.farmprogress.com/outlook/farmer-suicide-topic-few-will-discuss

Foote, R.H. (2002). The history of artificial insemination: selected notes and notables. American Society of Animal Science. Retrieved from https://www.asas.org/docs/default-source/midwest/mw2020/publications/footehist.pdf

Frey, M. (2021, May, 21). Milk nutrition facts and health benefits. Verywellfit.com. Retrieved from https://www.verywellfit.com/milk-nutrition-facts-calories-and-health-benefits-4117877#:~:text

Garnett, T. & Godde, C. (2017). Grazed and confused?Retrieved fromFood Climate Research Network:https://www.tabledebates.org/sites/default/files/2020-10/fcrn_gnc_report.pdf

Geiger, C. (2021, May). Could artificial insemination become illegal? Hoard's Dairyman. Retrieved from https://hoards.com/article-30153-could-artificial-insemination-become-illegal.html

Green, E. (2013, November 20). The controversial life of skim milk. The Atlantic. Retrieved from https://www.theatlantic.com/health/archive/2013/11/the-controversial-life-of-skim-milk/281655/

Green, T. (2017, January 29). Everyday birds—the blue tit [Web log post]. Everyday Nature Trails. Retrieved from https://theresagreen.me/tag/blue-tits-taking-milk-from-bottles/

Heuristic. (n.d.). In Merriam-Webster's online dictionary. Retrieved from https://www.merriam-webster.com/dictionary/carbon%20credit

Heuristic. (2021). Violent and graphic content. Facebook Community Standards. Retrieved from https://transparency.fb.com/policies/community-standards/violent-graphic-content/?from=https%3A%2F%2Fwww.facebook.com%2Fcommunitystandards%2Fgraphic_violence%2F

Hirst, K.K. (2019). Dairy farming–the ancient history of producing milk. ThoughtCo. Retrieved from https://www.thoughtco.com/dairy-farming-ancient-history-171199

Investopedia Team, The. (2021). What is Money? In R.C. Kelly (Ed.) Investopedia Education Economy (June 22, 2021). Retrieved from https://www.investopedia.com/insights/what-is-money/

Kanchwala, H. (2021, May 19). How did we start drinking milk of the ruminants? [Web Log post]. Science ABC. Retrieved from https://www.scienceabc.com/humans/species-drink-milk-another-species.html

Knothe, G., Krahl, J., & Gerpen, J. [Eds.]. (2010). The History of Vegetable Oil Based Diesel Fuels. In The Biodiesel Handbook, Second Edition. Urbana, IL: AOCS Press.

Lada, A., Wang, M., & Yan, T. (2021). How machine learning powers Facebook's new feed ranking algorithm, Facebook Engineering. Retrieved from https://engineering.fb.com/2021/01/26/ml-applications/news-feed-ranking/

Larkins, A. (2019). Infertility and abortions in cows. Agriculture and Food, Department of Primary Industries and Regional Development. Retrieved from https://www.agric.wa.gov.au/livestock-biosecurity/infertility-and-abortion-cows

Lee, K. (2011, February 27). Time management for dairy cows. Michigan State University. Retrieved from https://www.canr.msu.edu/news/time_management_for_dairy_cows

Lesser Prairie Chicken Initiative. (n.d.). LPCI overview [About page]. Retrieved from https://www.lpcinitiative.org/about/lpci-overview/

McLaren, P. (1984). D.C. Machines, In Brandon P. and Adby, P. (Eds.) Elementary Electric Power and Machines, (pp. 182–83). Chichester, U.K.: John Wiley & Sons. Retrieved from https://archive.org/details/elementaryelectr0000mcla/page/182/mode/2up

Melosi, M. (2010). The automobile and the environment in American history. Automobile in American Life and Society, University of Michigan–Dearborn and Benson Ford Research Center. Retrieved from http://www.autolife.umd.umich.edu/Environment/E_Overview/E_Overview3.htm

Mikus, T., Marzel, R., & Mikus, O. (2020). Early weaning: new insights on an ever-persistent problem in the dairy industry. Journal of Dairy Research, 87 (S1), 88-92. doi: S0022029920000503. Retrieved from https://www.cambridge.org/core/services/aop-cambridge-core/content/view/EBE6154104FA79B46421208CB62510AF/S0022029920000503a.pdf

Moran, J. & Doyle, R. (2015). Cattle Behavior. In Cow Talk: Understanding Dairy Cow Behaviour to Improve Their Welfare on Asian Farms (pp. 37-67). Clayton South VIC, Australia: CSIRO Publishing.

National Priorities Project. (n.d.). Chart: Total Federal Spending 2015: $3.8 Trillion [Chart]. Washington, D.C.: Office of Management and Budget. Retrieved from https://media.nationalpriorities.org/uploads/total_spending_pie%2C__2015_enacted.png

Natural Resources Conservation Service. (n.d.). Animal Feeding Operations. Washington, D.C.: United States Department of Agriculture. Retrieved from https://www.nrcs.usda.gov/wps/portal/nrcs/main/national/plantsanimals/livestock/afo/

Nauert, R. (2018). Why do we anthropomorphize? PsychCentral. Retrieved from https://psychcentral.com/news/2018/03/01/why-do-we-anthropomorphize#1

Noble Research Institute. (n.d.). What is the difference between organic and regenerative agriculture? Regenerative Agriculture. Retrieved from https://www.noble.org/regenerative-agriculture/organic-vs-regenerative-agriculture/

Oregon Secretary of State. (2020, November 2). Oregon changes to animal abuse, neglect, and assault law initiative: Petition 13. Retrieved from http://oregonvotes.org/irr/2022/013text.pdf

Pearce, L.E., Smythe, B.W., Crawford, R.A., Oakley, E., Hathaway, S.C.,&Shepherd, J.M. (2012). Pasteurization of milk: The heat inactivation kinetics of milk-borne dairy pathogens under commercial-type conditions of turbulent flow. Journal of Dairy Science, 95 (1). 20–35. doi:10.3168/jds.2011-4556

Pierson, T. (2014, August 15). Milk: The history and controversy [Web log post]. Dairy Council of Utah/Nevada. Also: permission to use via Personal Correspondence received October 4, 2021. Retrieved from http://dairyutnv.blogspot.com/2014/08/milk-history-and-controversy.html

Roach, K. (2021, June 10). Dr. Roach: Grass-fed beef not best source of omega-3 fatty acid. Saint Louis Post-Dispatch. Retrieved from https://www.stltoday.com/lifestyles/health-med-fit/health/to-your-good-health/dr-roach-grass-fed-beef-not-best-source-of-omega-3-fatty-acid/article_145a53b9-4bd2-5c78-9f77-2d1ad2be090e.html

Rosen, G. (2021, March 22). How we're tackling misinformation across our apps. Facebook Newsroom. Retrieved from https://about.fb.com/news/2021/03/how-were-tackling-misinformation-across-our-apps/

Rowell, T.E. (1974). The concept of social dominance [Abstract]. Behavioral Biology, 11 (2): 131–154. doi:10.1016/S0091-6773(74)90289-2. Retrieved from https://www.sciencedirect.com/science/article/abs/pii/S0091677374902892

Smith, P.W. (1981, August). Milk Pasteurization. Fact Sheet Number 57, United States Department of Agriculture Research Service, Washington, D.C.

Sovacool, B. K. (2011). Four problems with global carbon markets: a critical review. Energy and Environment, 22 (6). 681-694. doi: 10.1260/0958-305X.22.6.681. Retrieved from http://sro.sussex.ac.uk/id/eprint/58268/1/0958-305x%252E22%252E6%252E681.pdf

Stehulová, I., Lidfors, L., Spinka, M. (2007). Response of dairy cows and calves to early separation: effect of calf age and visual and auditory contact after separation. Applied Animal Behaviour Science, 110, 144-165. doi:10.1016/j.applanim.2007.03.028. Retrieved from https://slunik.slu.se/kursfiler/HV0041/10314.0910/Cow-calf_separation_at_different_ages.pdf

Surowiecki, J. (2021). A Brief History of Money. In IEEE Spectrum (May 30, 2021). Retrieved from https://spectrum.ieee.org/a-brief-history-of-money

Thomas, M. (2021, June 8). Does Instagram shadowban accounts? [Web log post]. Retrieved from https://later.com/blog/instagram-shadowban/

Thunnissen, D., Guernsey, C., Baker, R.,&Miyake, R. (2004). Advanced Space Storable Propellants for Outer Planet Exploration. American Institute of Aeronautics and Astronautics, 4, 28.

Todd, A. (n.d.). Traditions run 100-years deep at Tillamook County Creamery. Rural Cooperatives Magazine (July/August 2009). Retrieved from https://web.archive.org/web/20100123084628/http://www.rurdev.usda.gov/rbs/pub/jul09/tradition.htm

United Auto Workers Union (Producer). (2015). A brief history of theUAW [Video]. Retrieved from https://www.youtube.com/watch?v=nyb1sP6_wkk

United States Environmental Protection Agency. (n.d.). Sustainability primer (Issue brief No. 9). Washington, D.C. Retrieved from https://www.epa.gov/sites/default/files/2015-05/documents/sustainability_primer_v9.pdf

United States Environmental Protection Agency. (2021, April 14). Inventory of U.S. greenhouse gas emissions and sinks. Washington, D.C. Retrieved from https://www.epa.gov/sites/default/files/2021-04/documents/us-ghg-inventory-2021-main-text.pdf

United States Environmental Protection Agency. (2021, July 27). Sources of greenhouse gas emissions. Greenhouse Gas Emissions. Washington, D.C. Retrieved from https://www.epa.gov/ghgemissions/sources-greenhouse-gas-emissions

United States Environmental Protection Agency. (2008, August). Outdoor water use in the United States. EPA Water Sense, EPA-832-F-06-005. Retrieved from https://archive.epa.gov/greenbuilding/web/pdf/ws_outdoor508.pdf

University College London. (2012, March 27). DNA traces cattle back to a small herd domesticated around 10,500 years ago. ScienceDaily. Retrieved from https://archive.epa.gov/greenbuilding/web/pdf/ws_outdoor508.pdfwww.sciencedaily.com/releases/2012/03/120327124243.htm

Warner Lambert Co. vs United States, 343 F.Supp.2d 1315, 1320 (Ct. Int'l Trade 2004), rev'd (Fed. Cir. 2005). Retrieved from https://caselaw.findlaw.com/us-federal-circuit/1195577.html

Weary D.M., Chua, B. (2000). Effects of early separation on the dairy cow and calf1. separation at 6 h, 1 day and 4 days after birth. Applied Animal Behaviour Science, 69, 177-188. Retrieved from https://goveganworld.com/wp-content/uploads/2017/07/Weary-Effects-of-early-separation-of-dairy-cow-and-calf-PIIS01681591000001283.pdf

Welch, C. (2021, March 11). First study of all Amazon greenhouse gases suggests the damaged forest is now worsening climate change. National Geographic. Retrieved from https://www.nationalgeographic.com/environment/article/amazon-rainforest-now-appears-to-be-contributing-to-climate-change

Wernick, A. (2020, August 7). US lost 11 million acres of farmland to development in past 2 decades. The World. Retrieved from https://www.pri.org/stories/2020-08-07/us-lost-11-million-acres-farmland-development-past-2-decades

What do milk fat percentages mean? (2018, April 30). Undeniably Dairy News. Retrieved from https://www.usdairy.com/news-articles/what-do-milk-fat-percentages-mean

Wilcox, C. (2011, July 18). Mythbusting 101: Organic farming> conventional agriculture [Web log post]. Scientific American. Retrieved from https://blogs.scientificamerican.com/science-sushi/httpblogsscientificamericancomscience-sushi20110718mythbusting-101-organic-farming-conventional-agriculture/#

Wrigley, E., Corke, H., Seetharaman, K., & Faubion, J. [Eds.]. (2016). Encyclopedia of Food Grains, Second Edition. Waltham, MA: Academic Press. Retrieved from https://books.google.com/books?id=ce7tBgAAQBAJ&pg=PA238#v=onepage&q&f=false

Zahidul. (2020, February 11). Methods, Time, and Temperature for Pasteurizing Milk [Web log post]. Milky Day. Retrieved from https://milkyday.com/blog/2020/02/11/methods-time-and-temperature-for-milk-pasteurization/

Manufactured by Amazon.ca
Bolton, ON